$6.95

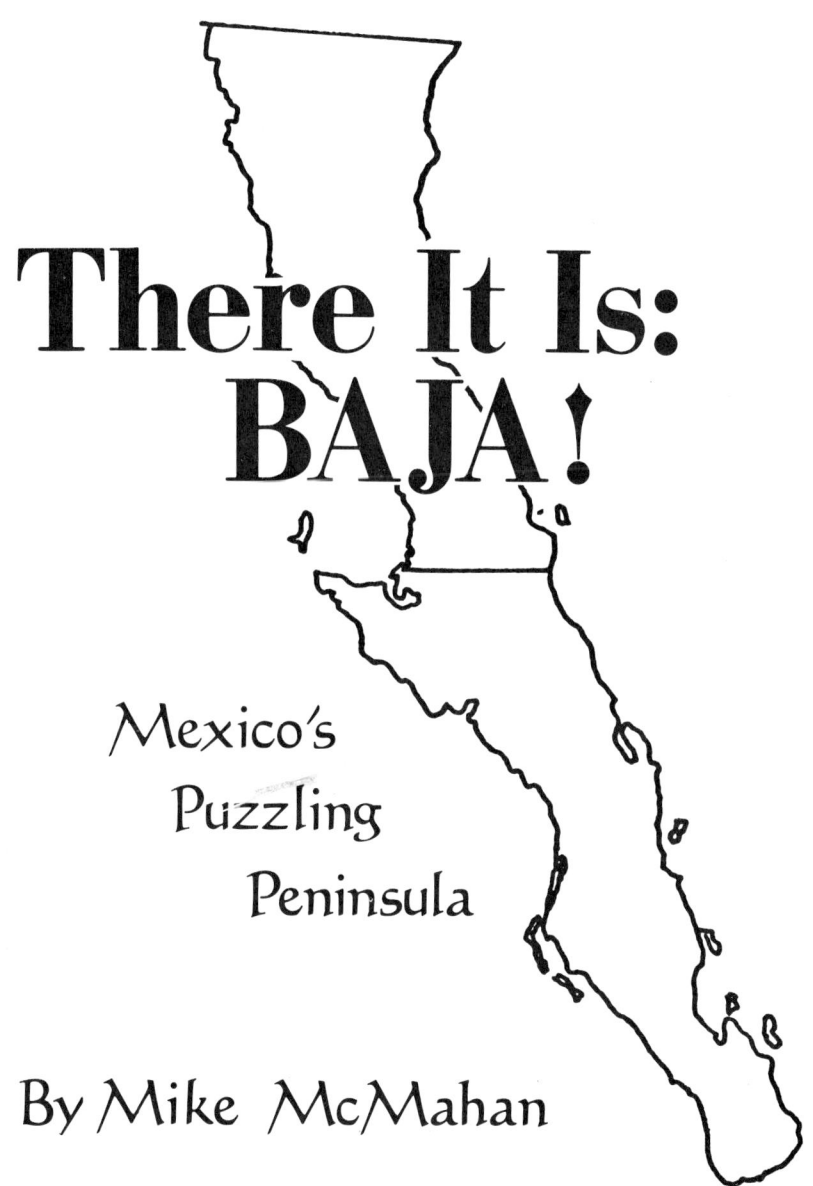

There It Is: BAJA!

Mexico's Puzzling Peninsula

By Mike McMahan

BROOKE HOUSE, NORTHRIDGE, CA

Library of Congress Catalog Card Number 71-172517
ISBN 0-910950-04-0
Printed USA
© 1973, 1974 By Mike McMahan
3131 South Figueroa, Los Angeles, Calif. 90007
(213) 747-4224
Second Edition 1974
All Rights Reserved

Reviewers may quote brief passages of 100 words or less without specific permission. Every consideration will be given requests for quoting longer passages, but written permission is required.

Dedication

To all the McMahan youngsters who "grew up" on these Baja trips:

To Pat, my son. To Ginger (Mary), Carol and Diana, my three daughters.

Great campers, all. Adventurers at heart. And when it came time to write this book, a great help all around. I'm proud of them.

I'm grateful too, for the rich experiences we've shared while exploring this magnificent peninsula; our trips have enriched all our lives and they remain, for each of us, an ever-pleasant memory.

Contents

Illustrations, Maps and Charts 9
Preface and Point-of-View 11
Acknowledgements 15
Foreword 16

1. DISCOVERY: New & Old, Fact & Fancy 23
    Hoei-Sin, in 499 B.C.   The Second Coming of Cortés
    Gold! And Amazon Women!   Tough Luck, Bitter Luck
    Island Called California   Say Something Nice
    Natives from Outer Space?

2. "MUY MACHO!" The Mexican Point-of-View 39
    Mexicans Hate Our Guts   Uncle Sam Grabs a Half
    Two Hot Bloods in One   Love Potions & Aphrodisiacs
    Heritage from the Past   "Muy Macho!"
    Comes the Revolution

3. SEA OF CORTEZ: Trampa Pescado Propia de Dios 53
    Genesis of a Peninsula   21 Varieties in a Single Catch
    What a Fish Trap!   105-Pounder in the Surf?
    800 Varieties — and Whales   How the Natives Do It
    Surf Fishing's My Favorite

4. TIJUANA: World's Busiest Border Crossing 71
    Gambling Mecca of the '20s   Adrenalin for Gambler's Blood
    The New Era, the New Lures   Olé! The Bull Fights!
    "La Mordida" — the Bite   Supermarketing for Inland
    The Horse Nuts

5. BAJA BY CAMPER TRUCK: Rugged Center Section 87
    The Three Parts of Baja   My Friend, the Fayuquero
    The Desert's a Killer, for Sure   Time in Baja Doesn't Run, It Strolls
    Four-Wheel Drive: "La Burrita"   Death in the Desert
    Special Check List for Baja

6. MALARRIMO BEACH: Loot for Beachcombers 103
    Junk Heap for the Pacific   Steamer Chairs — and Plane Wrecks
    By Sea, by Air?   A Chance to Dig History
    Tough Trek by Desert Road   Aschmann: Early Explorers
    There It Is: Malarrimo!

7. **TALE OF A WHALE: Scammon Lagoon** 115
    Where Whales Come to Play
    Sex and the Single Whale
    Captain Scammon's Secret
    Heartbeat of a Whale
    Historic "Kitchen Middens"
    Sea Shells for Collectors
    Steinbeck's "Pearl" — and a Philosophy

8. **MEXICAN INGENUITY: Tips on Lots of Things** 127
    Tips Around the Campfire
    Tips for the Road
    Fishing and Miscellaneous Ingenuity
    Dad Had a Trick or Two, Himself
    The Point of the Cactus
    Ingenuity with Language

9. **CAMPFIRE GOURMET: My Favorite Recipes** 141
    Ambiance by the Campfire
    Orégano Grows Wild
    How to Cook With Rocks
    Cornmeal Is a Flavor
    What to Do with Two Ducks
    Viva La Banana: The Baja Macho
    Beer for Breakfast?

10. **THE LAZY RESORTS: Travel to the Tip** 163
    "The Baja Week-End" by Air
    By Car and by Ferry
    Parallels: Honolulu, Acapulco
    The Food is Special
    How to Make a Margarita
    Damiana: The Aphrodisiac
    The Price is Right

11. **SKIN DIVING: My Son Pat, the Expert** 181
    Lobsters, East and West
    Pat on Native Techniques
    How to Find Where the Action Is
    Spearing the Sportfish
    Halibut, Abalone, Scallops, Clams
    Who's Afraid of Sharks?
    Jellyfish and Other Nuisances

12. **THE PERIPATETIC PADRES:**
    Fiestas, Frustrations, Footnotes 195
    Fiestas & Festivals
    25 Steps to Alta California
    The Ruins of Santa María
    Jesuits Out, Franciscans In
    The Indians Kill a Priest
    The Father Who Fathered a Village
    Pot of Gold in a Mission Wall

13. **PIRATES & PEOPLE: Strange Characters of Baja** 209
    The Buccaneers of Baja
    Cavendish, the British Pirate
    The Revolutionary Mr. Walker
    What's in a Name? "Ho-Nez . . ."
    Mi Amigo, Richard Daggett
    The Russians Colonize Baja
    The Americans Trick the British

14. **PERSONAL OBSERVATIONS:**
    25 Years a Baja Aficionado 223
    "Wetbacks": Millionaire Smugglers
    The Tempting New World of Tourist Money
    Peyote vs. Bourbon
    A New Geothermal Field
    Farmers and the State of the Onion
    The Irresistible Urge to Return

Selected, Annotated Suggestions for Further Reading 234

ILLUSTRATIONS, MAPS AND CHARTS

Color Illustrations

Mike Examines Rock Paintings Near La Paz	17
Maya Aristocrat; Mixtec Jewelry	27
Skin Diving Area; Sea Bass Caught Near The Tip	61
Campsite at Bahía Concepcíon; Puerto Chileno Bay	95
Loot From Malarrimo Beach	105
Whale Scene in Scammons Lagoon	114a
Mike With Rock Oven; Pat McMahan Displays Fish, Lobster	147
Space Photo, Lower Peninsula; Diana McMahan and Marlin	173
Mission San Javier, Mission San Borja	199

The text is also profusely illustrated with halftones from black and white photographs; these are too numerous to list here.

Maps and Charts

The Exciting World of Baja	6
Pre-Cortés Indian Tribes of Baja and The Gulf	31
Uncle Sam's Land Grab	40
Baja/Mexico Historical Map	45
Mike's 5 Favorite Fishing Spots	57
Mike's Fishing Chart	64
Population Estimate, 1974	73
Hunting Map	86
Rainfall Map	96
Air Transportation	164

Maps and Charts - Continued

Bus, Ferry, and Train Service 166

Present and Proposed Yacht Anchorages 168

Resorts and Inns, Lower Half of Baja 174

Lobster Map — Distribution of the Caribe and Pacific Spiny . .185

Path of The Missions and Mission Stations In Baja 198

The Mines of Baja 226

Preface and Point of View

Baja has been my mistress for twenty years.

A wench. Sometimes she's combined her worst features with the wrath of Mother Nature, and then she's really a bitch. But despite the rough times, she's still a young, exciting señorita, coming into the full of life. She is many things, my beautiful Baja.

Oh, she's not been true to me; many an adventurer has been there before me, and some have given her a bad name. But whether they explored her attractions just once — or even fifty times — they don't know her like I do.

I've come to know her many moods, her many faults. And her very special *ecstacies.* Those others — *caramba!* — they were the amateurs.

Take Cortés. He claims he "discovered" her — but he tried to steal her gold. She broke his heart, and sent him back a broken man, with little more than a sad tale to carry.

And the priests. They tried to make a "good woman" of her. But who should confess? One priest reportedly fathered a whole village and many of the townspeople still bear his name. Two priests were killed by Baja Indians.

The pirates? Baja gave them a tough time. The *banditos?* Short shrift. The American adventurer, William Walker, who proclaimed himself president of Baja? A funny story . . .

Oh, I know her like a book. This seductive señorita.

Baja is a bewilderness of things. Down her spine go those cruel and craggy mountains that whip up in the air like a scorpion's tail at the end of the American Rockies. And on the sides of canyon walls, you can search and find the primitive cave paintings of the Indians.

Farther down: pure pleasure. Tropical luxury, sunbrightened beaches of sparkle sand and lazy resorts to woo more lovers. That's where the marlin leap high and the crystal-clear coves and bays beckon one to return at end of day.

To the sunset's side is the wide ocean. Hidden there, Captain Scammon's secret lagoon where the 5,000 gray whales of the Pacific come each year for instinctive fun. A pair of these will make a sight you'll never forget. All 60 tons.

Then, Easterly, across the narrows of this peninsula, that fisherman's paradise: The Gulf of California. Some call it "The Sea of Cortez". Others: *"Trampa Pescado Propia de Dios"* — God's Own Fish Trap. For there Somebody trapped more than 800 kinds of fish, to make the second greatest sport I've found in all my born days. Fisherman's paradise. Cook's heaven.

And there's an island out in the Gulf where cannibals once had their friends for dinner.

When you stalk along a patch of sandy gravel, maybe you can *hear* an "upside down river" beneath your feet. Or suppose you drive your jeep over that arrogant *Viscaíno* Desert to *Malarrimo* Beach and find a beachcomber's treasure upon its treacherous sands. Here the broad Pacific has carried its flotsam and jetsam 9,000 miles to swirl at your feet. Old ships and shoes and whaling wrecks. And maybe a wave-tossed bottle of Scotch — on the rocks.

There were no maps of much of this when first I courted Baja. I had to make my own map — and, even now, this book has forced me to make a few new ones, just for you.

The airplane, you see, has changed it all. A hundred fifty trips ago, *"La Burrita"*, our jeep, wandered more than 1,000 miles to find land's end at the tip of Baja. And took three weeks.

Today, you jet it in a scant two hours — a straight 700 miles. So the arid desert in Baja's midriff has been leaped.

The airplane has unlocked secrets I really hadn't meant for every *loco turista* to know. And now the Mexican government and rich *aficionados* are spending a hundred million dollars to fancy up my Baja for more *turistas*.

Oh, well! Some of my exploring friends will rough it still, the first third of the way by car or through the desert by camper truck. In sleeping bag or tent — or air-conditioned room. Hmmmm! I knew her when . . .

So I'd better invite you now. *Mi casa es su casa!* My house is your house, even if you still bring your own sleeping bag. The camper's truck is fine. Or fly it, laze it in that lush resort, a frosty *Margarita* in your hand, a soft night's breeze teasing with the sweet perfume of tropic flowers.

— Or dream it in your armchair, traveler, and let me weave the warp and woof of this Christmas stocking that hangs there from our own California. Let's get to know this Baja mistress of mine.

There She Is: BAJA!

Bahía Concepción   Sherilyn Mentes

When Mike returns from one of his long trips to Baja, his beard reminds us of Ernest Hemingway.

Perhaps the raunchy flavor of the McMahan style doesn't match Hemingway's gift of language, but Mike has a singular dedication to his subject and a multidimensional perspective behind his point of view. He's brash, and sometimes a little belligerent. But always informative.

Mike's maps of Baja have been famous for years. He has explored the peninsula from end to end many times, and after 183 trips to almost every conceivable Baja destination, has possibly acquired a greater variety of experiences there than any other person in the world.

Mike's first book, the collaborative "Baja California," is now out of print. So is the exciting film short subject, "Mexican Duck Hunt," made nearly twenty years ago.

So his new book on Baja is most timely. There are new maps, new photographs, and endless nuggets of information tucked into this mother lode of Baja adventure he brings us.

And, always, there are Mike's irreverent footnotes — the salty, skeptical observations of a man who has *really* been there. Often. But never, as he says, often enough.

ENRIQUE SANTOYO
La Paz, Baja California
Mexico

Acknowledgements

I'm indebted to dozens of *Bajacalifornia* friends and *aficionados* for their assistance with this book.

Ray Haller was with me on my first *long* trip down the peninsula, more than a score of years ago; he's shared the camera work for many years. Other great hunting, fishing, and exploring companions were Tommy Foster, Dick Capp, George Mutter, Dick Shockley and my brother, Walter.

My son Pat contributed the information and experiences related in the chapter on Skin Diving. Ginger, my daughter, provided endless notes from her own trips with her husband, Chuck Potter.

Ralph Hancock and his staff came up with the research on Hoei-Sin and other items to back the text. Museums and newpapers from Mexico City to Los Angeles offered constructive suggestions and made thoughtful contributions.

Campbell Grant helped mightily in verifying the data on the petroglyphs (he's probably the foremost expert on primitive rocks). And Father Gabriel Chiodi also filled in a number of clues, leading to this petroglyph find. Father Chiodi, who was then at Guerrero Negro and now is at La Paz, is a very knowledgeable man, deeply interested in the early history of Baja.

Hugh Manessier, another great Baja aficionado, gave more authenticity to the manuscript by adding his own perspective to our final draft.

Finally, a bow to Blanche Cyne, who created the art for the "chapter symbols" along with other sketches and illustrations for the book.

To them all, my thanks.

Mike McMahan

Early Baja Stone Art Discovered by Mike

In 1972 and 1973, as the final chapters of this book were going into type, another "find" was uncovered in Baja by the author/explorer, Mike McMahan:

Hidden back in the hills in a sparse and now desolate part of the peninsula are these unique rock carvings and paintings — petroglyphs — that date back centuries to early Baja man.

Mike turned his photographs and data over to Campbell Grant, one of the foremost experts in the field of primitive rock art. (He is the author of "Petroglyphs and Rock Painings of Baja California" and "Rock Art of the American Indian".)

Grant recommended the exact location of the find not be disclosed by Mike until petroglyph experts could fully assess the data.

Above, one of the petroglyphs tells its own story of how the natives captured and killed their wild game: the two circles represent feathers on arrows.

Across, Mike examines the rock paintings found in another part of the peninsula some years earlier.

On a trip made since the publishing of the first edition, in November of 1973 Mike and a crew from Bill Burrud's TV show discovered another large new find of petroglyphs within two miles of the original location.

McMahan

Mike examines rock paintings at the area he first saw in 1970. Paintings are protected from the weather by the inward slant of the house-sized rock, which faces East. The area is south of La Paz and north of Punta Pescadores. Close-up, right, shows one of the paintings in detail; it is now known to natives as "The Man With Three Legs." It has been re-sketched below by a modern artist.

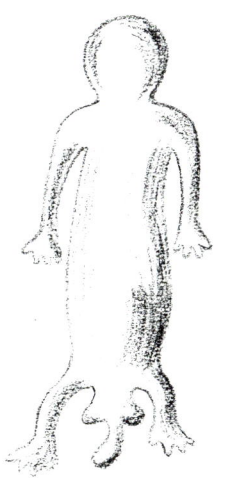

Mike McMahan

This petroglyph is somewhat similar in design to the painting shown in color on the other side. Here the figures have been pecked into the surface of the rock; the Indians apparently used whatever method best suited their interests at that particular time. This petroglyph is small in overall size; the phallic design is more prevalent in the southern part of the peninsula.

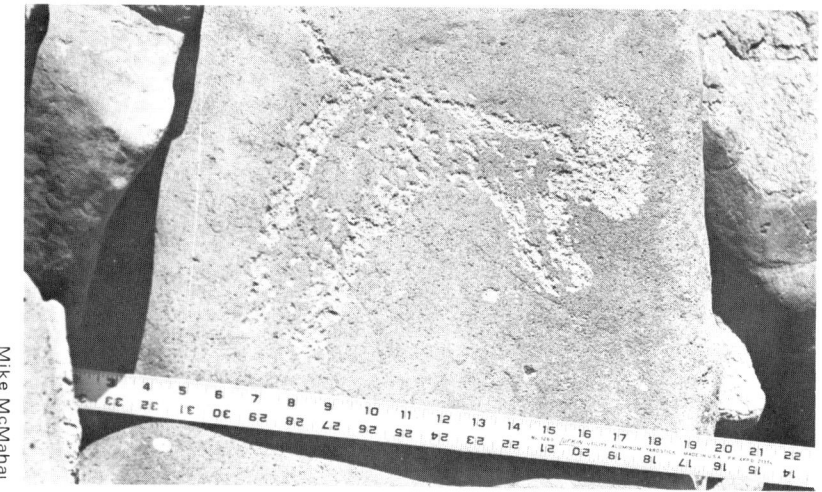

MORE THAN A THOUSAND ROCKS FOR HISTORY

Above, detail in a single stone with a yardstick to indicate the relative size.

Below, a general view. - - But it takes a second look to realize that this, indeed, was a virtual "art museum" in centuries past. Estimates on the rocks vary from 500 years back to before the birth of Christ. Generation after generation visited the "'museum" to add their individual contributions, scientists speculate.

At least a thousand petroglyphs are still to be found in the new area. Yet if one should pass this way, nothing would suggest that there was once human habitation in the locale.

THERE IT IS: BAJA!

Mike McMahan

CAN YOU SOLVE THE DESIGN PUZZLES?

As the experts attempt to decipher all the meanings behind the stone carvings, a better understanding of Baja's early inhabitants takes dimension. Here is one of the more baffling petroglyphs. Can you interpret the possible meanings?

Campbell Grant, in his analytical report to Mike after studying the photographs, has this to say:

"Historically this was the territory of the Cochimi Indians and there is no reason to believe that the rock art was not the work of these people. They were primarily hunters and gatherers, concentrating on the rabbit, deer, the Gulf of California, they harvested fish, shellfish and turtles.

"These were the items most often depicted in their paintings and carvings and the most likely reason for the many life-sized paintings of men and game animals was for the purpose of hunting or 'sympathetic' magic — the depiction of the animal would somehow aid in its capture. Often the animal is shown as pregnant and this could have been a fertility symbol to assure future game supplies.

"Design motifs include deer, rabbits, anthropomorphic figures (often impaled by arrows) fish, concentric circles, footprints, bighorn sheep, turtles, vulvas, and various abstract and geometric designs. The pictures are all pecked into the hard volcanic rock and the light inner rock surfaces provide the contrast to give a sharp negative effect."

*Campbell Grant is one of America's foremost experts in the field of primitive rock art and has written extensively about his specialty. For more information, refer to his 1965 book on "The Rock Paintings of the Chumash" and the 1967 edition of "Rock Art of the American Indian", and "Petroglyphs and Rock Paintings of Baja California", Baja California Symposium IX. Santa Ana 1971.

Bob DeVincent examines one of the petroglyphs at Mike's new area.

PERHAPS THE HIGH PRIEST?

While many of the petroglyphs are childlike in execution, experts are able to draw some intriguing theories and thoughtful conclusions from a study of the primitive art.

One expert insists the stone art above may represent a high priest. Snakes, vulvas and other symbolism abound, suggesting some of the same intertwining of sex and religion that is observed in the art of other races around the world.

Baja's natives may have been there 15,000 years ago, archaeologists surmise. When were they first discovered by more civilized man? - - That is also open to interesting conjecture. And that's where Mike's book begins:

Discovery:

New and Old,
Fact and Fancy

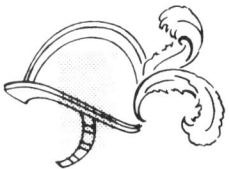

I. *Hoei-Sin, in 499 B.C.*
Gold! And Amazon Women!
"An Island Called California"
Natives from Outer Space?
The Second Coming of Cortés
Tough Luck, Bitter Luck
Say Something Nice

Maybe Hoei-Sin, the Buddhist monk from ancient China, really was the first explorer to set foot on Baja California.

So suggests the accounts of his travels to a strange new world in 499 B.C. And so it is recorded in the annals of China.

Today's scientists have now confirmed that there is an "ocean river" streaming across the broad Pacific where a branch of the Equatorial Current lands squarely on Baja. Even a wooden sandal floats 9,000 miles and hides amidst the beachcomber's trove at Malarrimo Beach.

Suppose Hoei-Sin rebuilt his ship there from the flotsam and jetsam he was sure to find?

And then he could have sailed on down the coastline to Baja's tip and caught the return current that later was to carry the Spanish galleons past the English buccaneering pirates and on beyond the Philippines. Could be.

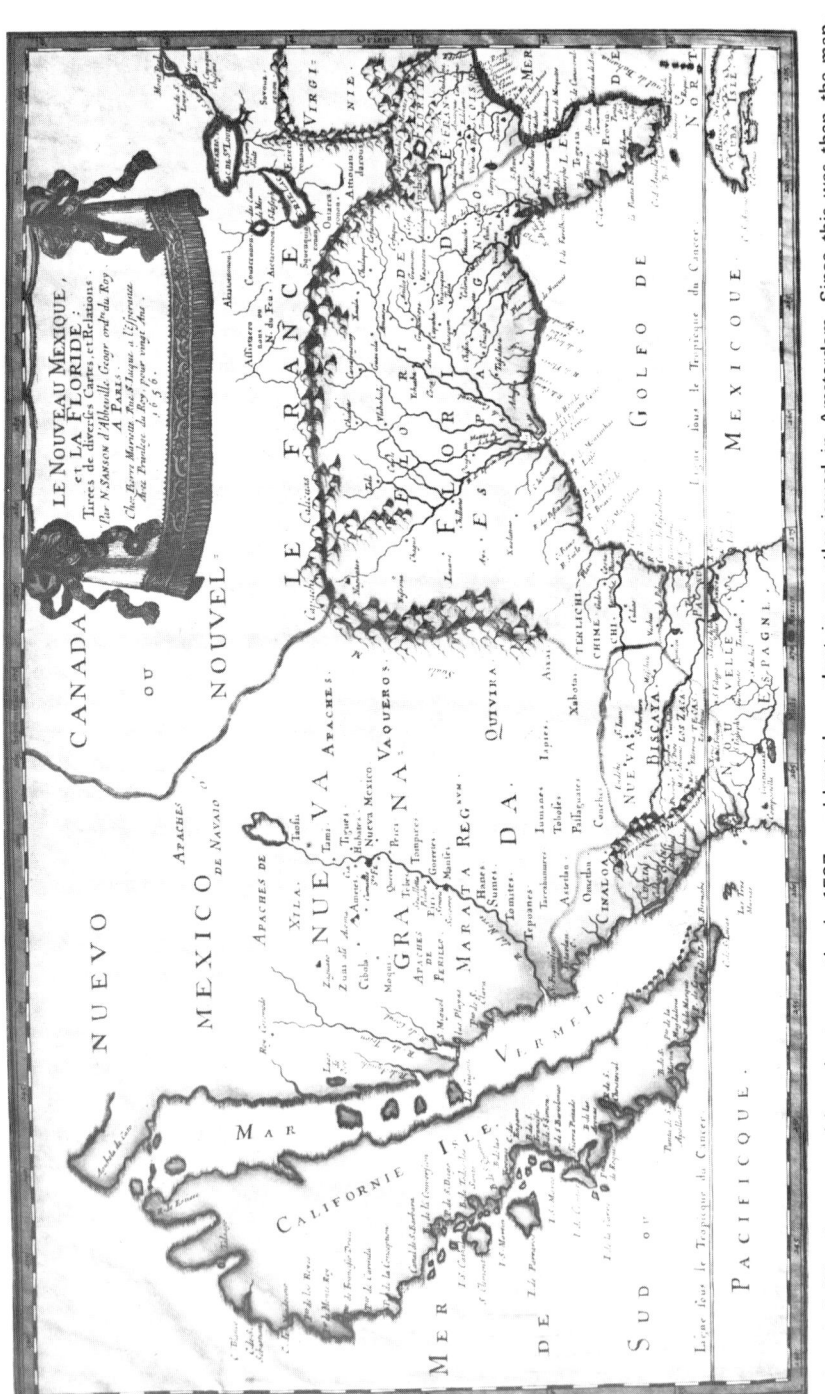

Courtesy of Bancroft Library, University of California, Berkeley.

Although California appeared in at least one atlas in 1597 as a blunted peninsula, the idea of California as an island began when a pilot named Morena so described it to Sir Francis Drake. By 1620, a Carmelite Priest (Antonio Ascension) had drawn his version showing California as an island, and sent it on to his superiors. Enroute to Spain, the ship carrying this chart was captured by Dutch pirates who must have been convinced of its authenticity; two years later it appeared as a printed chart in an atlas issued in Amsterdam. Since this was then the map-making center of the world, the chart was soon copied by English map-maker John Speed, and perhaps by others. The map shown here is dated 1656. Despite the fact that California had been proved to be a peninsula much earlier than 1747, it was not until that year that Spain finally issued a royal decree admitting that California was, after all, not an island.

Hoei-Sin would make Baja's discovery date about 25 centuries ago. You don't believe it? Then go along with all those who tab the date at 1535, when Hernando Cortés raised the flag for the Crown of Spain at Bahia de La Paz, and the peninsula — like its inhabitants — ceased to be a virgin land.*

So, maybe it was about 2,470 years ago. Surely, 437 years ago. With a place like Baja, someone was bound to find it.

Gold! And Amazon Women!

"Gold!" was the bright gleam in the eyes of Cortés, but there were also intriguing legends of a tribe of "Amazon women" that may have added a warmer glint to the eyeballs of his Spanish sailors.

Obviously, it wasn't hard to raise a crew with a sexy story like this: "Their arms are all of gold and so is the harness of the wild beasts they tame and ride. For in the whole island . . . there is no metal but gold . . . "

Island? Yes, early cartographers had imagined on their maps it was an island, not a peninsula. "An island . . . peopled by bronzed women," the early accounts dreamed on, "without any men among them, for they live in the fashion of the Amazons . . .

"All have strong, perfect figures, are ardent lovers and insatiable sex mates . . . "

Caramba, Hernando, how large a crew do you want!

Half the world was unexplored then. And half the world today can just as readily believe there is sex-life on Mars and that the adventurous will conquer it if only NASA doesn't run out of money.

Spain, too, amidst its many wars, was depleting its regal treasury of all that plundered gold from Mexico and Peru. Now to gamble that there must be more to the West! The *Conquistadores* had new worlds to conquer.

---

*The sailors saw to that . . .

"An Island Called California . . . "

An imaginative fictioneer of Spain's sixteenth century writers helped the gamble along with his vivid account of that fabulous Amazonian tale.

Garci Ordoñez de Montalvo was his name, and he created the character, "Esplandian," to be the adventurous hero. The Spanish readers loved it.

Esplandian, as Ordoñez conjured up the tale early in the 1500's, followed on the heels of Columbus to the New World and went on to "an island called California . . . very close to the Terrestrial Paradise . . . "

So Cortés had a pretty good breeze blowing from such an adventure yarn to fill the sails of those two new ships he was even then building on the West coast of Mexico's mainland. The Californias — *Baja y Alta,* Lower and Upper, *Antigua y Nueva,* Mexican and American — were about to be discovered.

Los Angeles and San Francisco were to come much later. And "Gold!" would start the Westward-Ho rush, another three centuries after that. But it all began, long before Walt Disney and President Ronald Reagan*, down there near the Tip of what we now call "Baja" — the first of the Californias.

The Natives Came from Outer Space?

The Indians were maybe 10,000, maybe 15,000 years before all this, of course. The natives. The aborigines.

And where did the Indians come from? Well, Baja offers you three theories, outside of the Adam-and-Eve story:

1. They came over with Hoei-Sin on the Equatorial current from China. No?

2. They came down — Along with other Indian tribes in

---

*President, Screen Actor's Guild, 1947-52; 1959-60. For other presidential aspirations, see your current newspaper.

This Maya aristocrat was proud, flamboyant. Olmec, Aztec, and Toltec cultures also contributed to Mexico's heritage.

Mexican National Tourist Council

Museum of Anthropology, Mexico City

Cortes discovered Mexico in 1519, stole its gold and enslaved the people. Although this Mixtec jewelry survived the plunder of Cortes, many works of art were destroyed when they were melted down to make bars of gold.

Mike McMahan

GIANT BAJA AMMONITE: MAYBE 65,000,000 YEARS

More than 18" in diameter, this coiled reminder of the ancient past completely dwarfs a modern soft drink bottle. These extinct mollusks have recently been discovered in Northern Baja near Santa Catarina. If these ammonites had been located in the United States, the odds could be much better that they would have been discovered a century or more ago. But despite the proximity of the peninsula to major cities of both Mexico and our country, much of Baja remains "unexplored" in a way that is unusual in the modern world. Although it seems likely that virtually every inch of Baja California was explored by the Indians, it is still possible that modern visitors — with adequate backgrounds in their fields of interest — can make discoveries that add to our knowledge of Baja's fascinating history.

exploding population steps — from Asiatic progenitors, around the Aleutians and down some Stone Age Alaskan highway. Too traditional?

3. Okay ... how about a far-out theory? In his book, *"Erinnerungen an die Zukunft,"* Erich von Däniken suggests that Mexico's remarkable Mayan culture may have been stimulated* by astronauts landing from another planet.

How else to explain this jet-propelled Mayan "astronaut" carved in stone in Mexico's ancient Palenque? And, coincidentally, what do you make of the old Mayan legend that tells of a "giant eagle" swooping down from the sky to land on earth: the eagle's beak opens and "four creatures" step out ...

ANCESTOR OF MAYAN MEXICANS ARRIVES BY JET?

In the National Museum of Anthropology, Mexico, there is a replica of this ancient stone carving found in a Mayan burial pyramid at Palenque, in the Mexican jungle. First discovered in 1952, the mystery is still unsolved. Does it represent a jet-propelled spacecraft? Is this some astronaut from another planet with advanced intelligence for Maya?

---

*And, obviously, cross-pollinated.

Is this a clue to the super-intelligence of the Indians of Mexico as they developed astronomical observatories, discovered the mathematical "zero" and perfected a 365-day calendar more accurate than the Julian calendar of Europe?

And did the Mayans, the Olmecs, the Toltecs and the Aztecs of Mexico's mainland have any influence on the tribes of Baja?

Anthropologists hypothesize there was human life on Mexico 20,000 years ago. Baja? Maybe 15, but the tribes burned their dead, so there's nothing left for a carbon-14 test.

Yet tests of the charcoal of their ancient fires indicate that someone was around at least 7,000 years ago, learning the tricks of a California barbecue.

At any rate, the civilization on the peninsula bears no traces of the be-templed, be-pyramided heights reached by the Mayans and the Aztecs on the mainland. Worse, by the time of the arrival of Cortés, the Baja Indians had become a sorry lot.

None had learned to turn a wheel or cultivate the soil and only a few could weave a basket or make pottery. There wasn't too much need, perhaps. There was food enough to eat: shell-fish, wild berries, sparser small game you could kill with a rock. Enough.

They were simple children in the sun.

The Second Coming of Cortés

So this is what lay in store for Cortés. No Amazons. No gold. Not even a village at La Paz — where Destiny had booked his landing.

Little did Cortés and his lusty sailors realize just what was ahead as they built those two boats at Tehuantepec.*

---

*An Indian word meaning "mountain of the man eaters." Tehuantepec is located on the river of the same name, some 300 miles east of Acapulco.

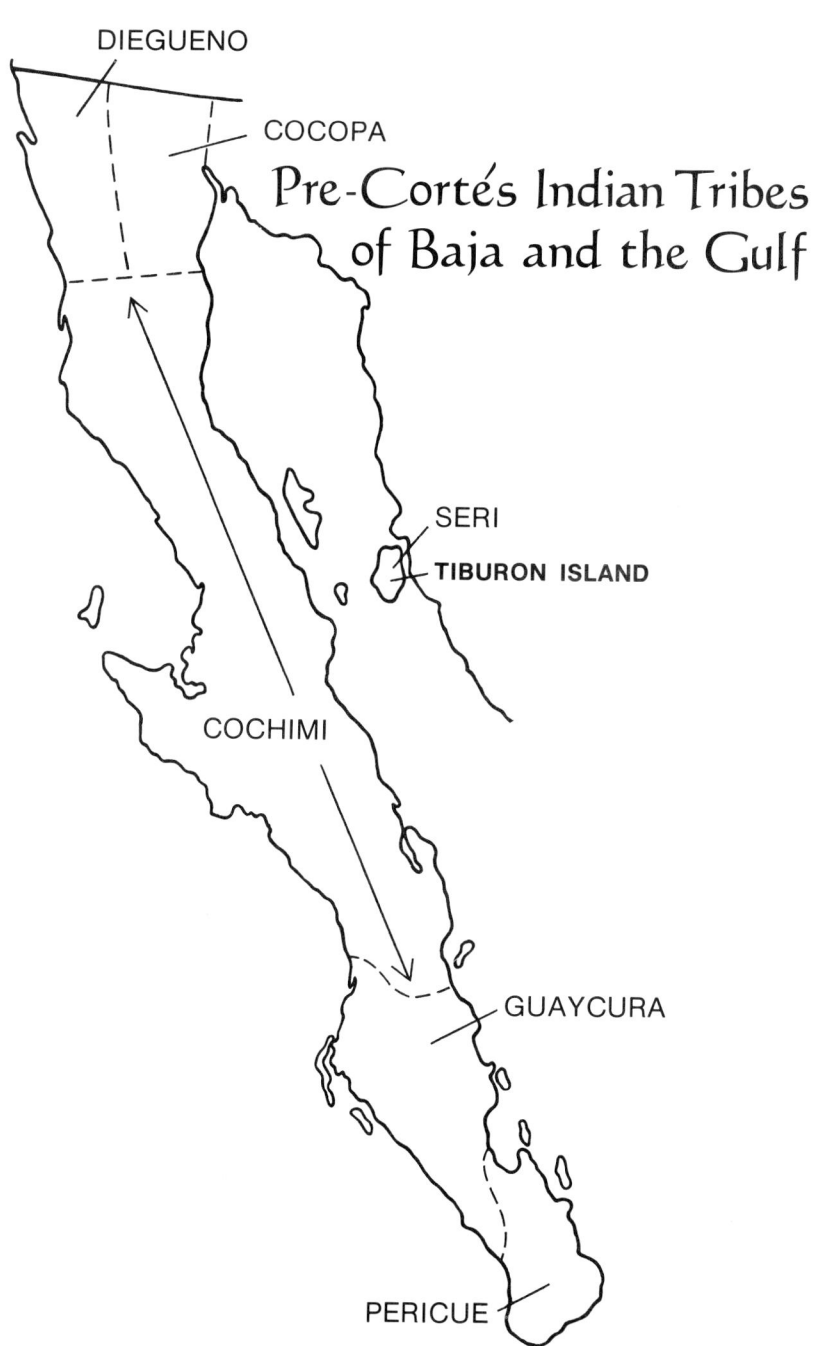

Mike McMahan

CONTRASTS OF BAJA

Baja is many landscapes, many temperatures. The center of the peninsula has the Viscaíno Desert. The lower part is more lush, tropical. Above: a jackrabbit seeks the scant shade of desert shrubs. Below: vegetation thrives at Mulegé.

Ray Haller

In fact, Cortés had almost more trouble than he could handle. Following the early glories of his complete conquest of Mexico in three short years — from 1519 to 1521 — he had returned to Spain to find conniving enemies confronting him at court. Much of his former power with the Crown had been emasculated.

It took extended engagements at court to win back his honor and prestige for a new try.

At last he was cleared. After all, Spain wanted more gold. Cortés had found some in Mexico and swore there would be more gold to the West. Why, look — you could see it in the sunset . . .

As the two ships set sail across what would soon come to be called "The Sea of Cortés," the now aging explorer found himself circumstantially detained on land.

Cortés was lucky, indeed; the crew of one ship mutinied, and murdered its unlucky Captain Becerra. When the pilot Jiménez and the rest of the murderous crew landed at La Paz, the Indians in turn massacred them. The second ship was separated from Becerra's ill-fated vessel of death the first night out of Tehuantepec, and returned to Acapulco months later having discovered only the deserted Revilla Gigedo Islands, some 300 miles south of the peninsula.

Cortés, at Tehuantepec, immediately ordered three more ships built and, this time, headed the expedition himself.

He landed at La Paz on May 3, 1535, and took possession in the name of Spain. Baja was officially "discovered . . ."*

Cortés ordered a fort established and stayed to supervise the building. Back went the ships to the mainland for more provisions, more supplies and a quorum of colonists.

Tough Luck, Bitter Luck

More tough luck. A *chubasco,* that violent summer/fall storm

---

*Keep in mind that this was still 85 years before the Mayflower ran out of beer and landed the Pilgrims at Plymouth Rock.

that sometimes disturbs the tranquility of Baja waters (I know, I barely lived through one 416 years later — 1939), smashed one of the ships and its load of colonists on the shores of Jalisco on the Mexican mainland.

The other ship brought not enough provisions, not enough colonists to support Cortés in the style to which he hoped to become accustomed.

More tough luck. Half those not-enough colonists were to die of hunger the first year. Had they only had the gumption to twist up a fishhook they could have survived grandly on the wealth of seafood about them.

Along with other problems, the explorers managed to pass along their quiescent forms of venereal disease, malaria, smallpox and measles to the inhabitants. Even as Columbus' crew had contrived to spread their "European plagues" to their welcoming parties on more Eastern shores.

The diseases raged virulently in new containers as sex traded back and forth. The native Indian population of Baja was destined to be decimated from 75,000 to a mere 7,000.

As for the colonists, the half who survived hunger and those extracurricular exploratory endeavors, had still more tough luck in store. Says one report, "The rest suffered likewise from ill-health and cursed Cortés, the island, the bay and this discovery."

Meanwhile, Cortés was doing a little cursing on his own. His evaluation of the native indians, as sent back to Spain, was at some odds with Esplandian's promises, " ... Perfect savages, (they) neither grow maize nor in any way till the ground, but merely live on wild fruits, fish and animals."

So the sunset's dream darkened into a nightmare. And Cortés and his now less-than-faithful survivors went back to the mainland. A modern writer, Ray Cannon*, has done much to keep the memory warm and thoughtful by titling his book, "The Sea of Cortez." But, otherwise, Hernando** left little legacy west of the mainland for history to footnote.

*A good guy, but incurably romantic.
**A bad guy. Even today, Mexico gives him no statue.

Other expeditions by other explorers followed. But none came back with as much as a souvenir postcard. No Amazons. *No oro!* No gold.

Then Came the Jesuits

"Everything concerning California is of such little importance that it is hardly worth the trouble to take a pen and write about it."

So wrote the Jesuit missionary who became noted for his criticism of the peninsula and its primitive inhabitants.

"Of poor shrubs, useless thorn bushes and bare rocks, of piles of stones and sand without water or wood, of a handful of people who beside their physical shape and ability to think, have nothing to distinguish them from animals . . ."

Father Johann Jakob Baegert had spent 17 years there when he wrote that and, just possibly, this report is what gave Baja its title, "The Land That God Forgot."

At any rate, the Jesuits and later the Franciscans and the Dominicans were to have endless soul-searing misadventures as they patiently, unrewardingly, established their outpost missions up the lonely peninsula. Ahead was a more promising land where their missions would some day share the Alta California landscape with such other tourist monuments as Disneyland, Knott's Berry Farm, and 20th-Century Fox Studios.

But, in Baja, 37 tries proved the tasks of the missionaries almost impossible. Nearly all their food had to come from the mainland and they could produce no gold and few tangible goods in return. It was a barren, tough luck country and in the end even the priests joined in giving Baja the bad mouth.

Visitors Should Say Something Nice

Cortés disliked Francisco de Ulloa, who carried on the expeditions after Hernando sailed back to die in misery, unhappy and ignored.* Before Ulloa disappeared into a mist somewhere off

---

*He had plenty of reasons to be unhappy. The Baja venture had cost him 300,000 ducats of his own money.

the coast of California, his last words included this scorching indictment of Baja: "Of the four elements that comprise the universe, God gave this country only two: air and fire."

It was true. Water was almost as hard to come by as gold.

Alarcón explored the Gulf to discover the mouth of the Colorado river in 1540. Cabrillo sailed up the west side of the peninsula and discovered San Diego Bay in September, 1542.

And neither had a kind word for Baja.

An American reporter, J. Ross Browne, three centuries later — in 1863 — recounted his trip for *Harper's New Monthly Magazine:*

"All the vegetation visible to the eye seems to conspire against the intrusion of man. Every shrub is armed with thorns . . . the cactus tortures the traveler with piercing needles and remorseless fangs. Burrs with barbed thorns cover the ground . . . the very grass, wherever it grows, resents the touch with wasp-like stings that fester in the flesh . . . "

Browne also had a few nasty things to say about Baja's snakes and insects and skunks. And then winds up with his own endorsement of the Spanish viewpoint: " . . . accursed of God!"

Accursed of God? My sainted aunt!

— Don't you believe it!

Not my Baja! Let me, at long last, put these scurrilous rumors to rest and clear the name of this good woman with whom I've slept so many times. I speak for Baja.

Maybe the Jesuits and the great Cortés were dreaming of more gold than the church and the crown had a right to expect. Maybe Esplandian had been fictioned too much. And, just possibly, the writer for Harper's suffered so much discomfort during his travels in Baja California that he couldn't appreciate the varied charms of this awesome but barren peninsula.

DISCOVERY

For Baja is many things. The desert is not for the tenderfoot. The plush resort is not for the camper explorer. So shuffle the cards again, dealer. There's the challenge and excitement of a lifetime of satisfactions just dangling there on that peninsula.

It could be, in fact, a Christmas stocking . . .

Museum of Anthropology, Mexico City

MEXICAN SCULPTURE, 3,000 YEARS AGO

This huge, 16-ton monolithic head was carved by the Olmecs of Mexico nearly thirty centuries ago. The Olmecs, on the Gulf of Mexico, were long before the Maya and Aztec cultures, and also ahead of any significant work of American Indians.

Cal Karr

Until a few years ago, the Seri Indians considered Isla Tiburon as their homeland and they lived more isolated and primitive lives. Tiburon is located in the upper third of the Gulf near the mainland, and east of Bahia de Los Angeles. Now the Seris have moved to the mainland, and although they are still near Tiburon they are more exposed to modern influences. This young Seri displays some shells made into jewelry, but his hat and shirt are obviously products of the Mexico of today.

"Muy Macho!"

The Mexican
Point-of-View

2. *Mexicans Hate Our Guts*
Two Hot Bloods in One
Heritage from the Past
Comes the Revolution
Uncle Sam Grabs a Half
Love Potions & Aphrodisiacs
"Muy Macho!"

Mexicans hate our guts.

They should.

The gringo* has given the Mexican a rough time for the last hundred and fifty years. And Spain did the same for three centuries before that.

U.S. encouraged the Texas War of Independence (1836) and then we trumped up a full scale war of our own (1846).

---

*"Gringo" is Mexican slang for Americans. It probably started in our War of 1846 as American soldiers marched across the Rio Grande singing "Green Grow the Rushes, O". Hmmmmm: "greengrow . . ."

THERE IT IS: BAJA!

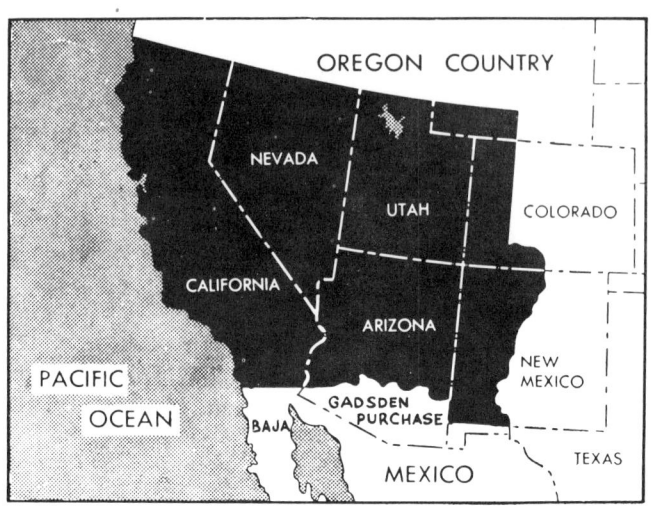

UNCLE SAM'S LAND GRAB: 5¢ AN ACRE ...

These were the spoils of war: Mexico agreed to sell more than 724,850 square miles of its land to U.S. — at a price that figured out to less than a nickel an acre! Meanwhile, we had annexed Texas. Total land: more than half of Mexico.

Between the two, United States took *more than half* of Mexico's land. In addition to Texas, our spoils included:

>California, all of it.
>Nevada, all of it.
>Utah, all of it.
>Arizona, most of it.
>New Mexico, most of it.
>And parts of Colorado and Wyoming ...

We increased the area of the United States by 792,339 square miles of Mexico's land, leaving them with their 760,373 today.

True, we paid a face-saving token of $15,000,000 for the land. (That was about *five cents an acre*).

And we got back — in just the next *ten* years — $600,000,000 in gold from California *alone*. Gold had been discovered there even before we signed the treaty.

Baja was not included. Upper California we wanted. It had gold. *Si!* Lower California? Cortés broke his heart there. Why should we? *No!*

How's that for adding insult to injury?

Two Hot Bloods for One

It is not surprising that the Mexicans hate our guts. Oh, not all of them. Some of them — the ones who understand the tragedy of their own bloody history. A hundred years has worn off some of the bitterness, but many inconsiderate American *turistas* keep picking at old wounds.

That's what I want to talk to you about, gringo, and see if I can't get you to help. I don't want you to be just another slob to my friend, the Mexican.

He is really a unique individual, the product of History's harsh and quixotic catalytic action over four and a half centuries. Two hot bloods in one.

Go back to the heritage of the Brilliant Maya civilization of fifteen centuries ago, or trace on back to the Olmec culture of 1000 B.C. Spice it with Toltec and Aztec civilizations. Then mix it with the European strains of the cruel Spaniards.

And what have you? *Trouble,* for one thing.

Now, don't make the mistake of thinking the Mexican is a Spaniard just because he speaks Spanish. Not so. Are Americans like their English forebears?

The Mexican really has good reason to hate the Spanish, too. They enslaved him and robbed him for 300 years before America got into the act.

The French also went to war on Mexico, and made it a "French Empire" in 1864 with an unemployed Austrian archduke to rule them. That was Maximilian II. He ended up in front of a Mexican firing squad three years later.

It has taken a lot of firing squads, assassinations and revolutions to get Mexico out of its violent past and into its promising future. It was a rough childhood. The Mexican had to learn to fight back and to stand on his own.

If the U.S. was to be its only friend, Mexico soon learned it needed no more enemies.

Heritage from the Past

Long, long before the Spanish came a-conquering in 1519, lusting for gold and silver, Mexico had a civilization that equaled and surpassed many aspects of Old World knowledge. The Maya had invented the abstract mathematical zero long before the rest of the world. These Indians devised a 365-day calendar that was far more accurate than the Europeans' Julian calendar. They had discovered a "penicillin" magic cure.

Astronomical observatories adorned their pyramids.*

Tenochtitlan (now Mexico City), the Aztec capital that welcomed Cortés, was *twice* the size of London then. And it was so clean and orderly the Europeans could scarcely believe it . . .

But know that these Aztecs were a bloodthirsty lot. Human sacrifice was the key to their entreaties to the Sun, the Rain God or any of the other four dozen deities they worshipped. And a winning warrior claimed his captive's haunches for steaks.

The God of Springtime was wooed and welcomed with a dance in the skin . . . a priest's dance in the just-removed skin of a victim . . .

Blood ran, red and often, on their magnificently designed sacrificial stones. The supreme prayer was made with the priest holding high to the sky a still-throbbing heart torn from a human chest. Their warriors cherished such an end as their own. The people accepted it as a religion. Their enemies came to fear it as their fate.

---

*Perhaps, indeed, as von Däniken suggests, there had been a little cross-pollination with visiting astronauts from another planet.

Before the Aztecs, the Maya (300-1200 A.D.) had a more intellectual culture, less war-like, certainly more restricted in sacrificial rites. Oh, a Maya maiden might get tossed into the Sacred Well at sunrise* to appease an inattentive Rain God. Of course, Mexican Indians were very dependent upon rain, as they had been tilling the fields and growing corn for two thousand years, already.

Before the Maya, the Olmec culture (1000 B.C. - 500 A.D.) had flourished in Mexico and their huge statues, as large as 50 tons, still speak of their creative glory. And they had their own written language.

The Olmecs worshipped the man-jaguar, half-human, half-cat — almost Chinese in its picturization. Perhaps Hoei-Sin had brought it across the Pacific . . . ?

Another, later civilization was the Toltec, which was flourishing about 900 A.D. One of their deities was Quetzalcoatl, the Feathered Serpent God, and thereby hangs our tale of Cortés.

Toplitzen, a Toltec high priest of Quetzalcoatl, had opposed the blood-letting excesses, worked piously and led a celibate life. That is, until his conniving enemies tricked him, got him inebriated with the King's sister and he lost his chastity, along with his right to stay around. He went into exile, disappearing into the East — but promising "Quetzalcoatl" would return. He even specified the date, some centuries hence.

A Strange Conquering, It Was

Cortés was to become, in the religious/superstitious thinking of the Aztecs, this reincarnation of Quetzalcoatl. The year, even as predicted, was 1519, the "Year of 13 Rabbits."

How else could this little band of 514 Spanish soldiers of fortune conquer a nation of 11,000,000 people?

The Aztecs sent out a welcoming party with gifts of gold and

---

*If she lived until noon, she received a reprieve. And she was expected to report on any chitchat with the Rain God about weather.

20 beautiful maidens, which whetted their appetites for more of both. The Spaniards marched on the capital, enlisting disgruntled Indian tribes along the way.

There was help from Malinche, the bright young Indian girl* whom Cortés picked from the 20. She learned Spanish, became his interpreter, his tactical adviser and incidentally, bore him a son.

Malinche told him of the Quetzalcoatl legend. He quickly saw the potentials of the role. And she told him there were many conquered tribes that might be encouraged to revolt against the Aztecs.

Moctezuma II (not "Montezuma", as our Marines mistakenly sing in "Halls Of — "), was the Aztec king, brave but foolish. His belief in the legend was confirmed in his mind as his fast-runner reports from Vera Cruz told him of the god-like, handsome, bearded, young (34) Cortés astride his horse. A supernatural warrior on four legs!

The entrance to Tenochtitlan was easy. The entire conquest seemed accepted as Cortés made the emperor Moctezuma a willing captive. In time, the lesser chieftans revolted; in the bloody slaughter which resulted, Moctezuma was killed and many soldiers under Cortés were drowned or killed as they retreated from the city with their plundered booty, an estimated 8 tons of gold.

With reinforcements, Cortés returned and won the city. More than 240,000 Aztecs were murdered in the 80-day siege. In all, it had taken only two years to subjugate 11,000,000 people and, in the next 80 years, 8,000,000 more were to die. From Slaughter. From the ravages of smallpox and the European diseases to which the Indians had no natural resistance. And from overwork in the slave labor of the gold and silver mines.

The Spaniards also were obliterating the vital traces of Aztec, Toltec, Maya and Olmec heritage, as quickly as they could. Even the books of the Maya (what stories these might have told!) were considered as being counter to the new "march of Christianity" and were ordered destroyed by the Catholic Bishop Diego de Landa.

*Hence, today, the Mexicans say of a traitor, "malinchista", as we would say "a benedict arnold" or Norweigans would say "a quisling".

Spain's Brand of Colonialism

The ruling class of the new country were the *Gachupínes* ("wearer of the spurs"), the Spanish/Spanish born in Spain.

Their Spanish/Spanish children, born in Mexico, were called *Criollos* ("creoles"). And these were to own many of the estates and mines, but rarely would they be permitted to participate in the government.

Next down the line, in pecking order, came the *Mestizos,* the Spanish/Indians. Spain's colonial policy encouraged interbreeding with the natives to provide a "buffer" group.

Soon hatred and revolt — the bastards of oppression — were breeding along with the Spaniards. By the 1800s, the *Mestizos* had grown to 2,000,000. And the *Criollos* to 1,000,000.

Spain was having her troubles at home. King Ferdinand VII had been tricked and captured by Napoleon. Mexico decided the time had come for revolt. Independence from Spain was declared September 16,* 1810.

The wars of independence went on for eleven bloody years. A million people were killed as faction turned on faction. Finally, the Spanish viceroys were banished once and for all in 1821. And it was exactly three hundred years after the Spanish discovered Mexico.

But yet another hundred years of slavery and oppression were in store as the *Criollos* seized command. Tyrants and dictators were to bleed the country even more. On all fronts, the Mexican was to be harrassed, exploited, challenged. Spain. United States. France. Even the Church.

The Church owned *half* the property and buildings in Mexico and, some say, had mortgages on much of the other half. It took in more money than the state.

The United States, to the North, offered little help. In fact, historians now reproach America's continuing secret maneuvers, both politically and commercially.

*National holiday. On the eve of September 16 now, you'll still hear the cry, "Death to the Gachupínes!"

Texas History, Slightly Revised

Mexico's Texas, settled mostly by Americans, wanted independence. The Texans had sided with Santa Anna in his bid for power in Mexico City, then revolted against him. Moot point: I studied Texas history when I was growing up in that Lone Star State — and it's taken quite a few years to get my brain rinsed out and put in perspective.

Let's just report that Texas won her independence in 1836. Santa Anna* had martyred the Alamo and massacred Goliad, but the Texans captured him in his afternoon siesta at San Jacinto.

Mexico refused to recognize Texas as a nation. England and France flirted with it, but the United States finally annexed it in 1845. Texas was the key to the new U.S. political cry of "Manifest Destiny!" as the States determined to extend their lands all the way to the Pacific.

On May 13, 1846, Congress declared war on Mexico. Texans claimed the Mexicans had fired on them. Mexicans said the Texans were on Mexican property. (Abraham Lincoln, for one, was later to question what we did.) No matter.

Our armies rolled. One swept to California. Another to New Mexico. Another crossed the Rio Grande. General Winfield Scott** (old "Fuss and Feathers" himself), landed at Vera Cruz and marched on Mexico City. The final battle was at Fort Chapultepec as schoolboys sacrificed their lives in a last-ditch defense.

West Point's finest graduates received campaign experience here to prepare for our own Civil War: Grant, Sherman, McClellan and Taylor; Robert E. Lee, "Stonewall" Jackson and Jefferson Davis.

At last, the "peace treaty" gave us land all the way from Texas to California, with Nevada and Utah thrown in.

---

*Santa was a one-legged General at that time. When his leg had been shot off in an earlier battle, he had it enshrined in the Cathedral in Mexico City. Holy Tibia!

**One of my ancestors, I apologetically admit.

Excepting Baja which, as usual, *nobody* wanted. This in spite of the fact that U.S. Troops had captured *Mulegé*, well down the peninsula. Correction: maybe it was *because* of the fact: *They saw Baja!*

Uncle Sam Grabs a Half

This gave the United States more than half of Mexico's original territory. Later we added a section to round off Arizona and New Mexico — the Gadsden Purchase — and paid $10,000,000 more.

Total, for half of Mexico: $25,000,000. Is it surprising the Mexican has a doubt or two about our "good neighbor" policy?

The internal problems below the Border continued, with dictatorships now in charge. Treachery, corruption, graft were the order of the day. One U.S. Ambassador was seriously implicated, and the oil interests and gringo land owners played strange and devious games. Before the end of the last century, foreigners — mostly Americans — would manage to gain ownership of 78% of Baja and much of the mainland. Already the Mexicans were sensing our moves and anti-gringo sentiment was growing.

It was the Americans who first backed Pancho Villa, then rejected him for Carranza. Villa retaliated by killing 18 American engineers and staging a raid on Columbus, N.M. We sent in General "Blackjack" Pershing to get Villa.

From 1910 to 1920, revolutions flared. Never since the Aztecs had so much blood been spilled. Leader fought leader, bandits fought bandits, and president after president was overthrown. Madero, Carranza, Villa, Zapata and Obregon were all to meet assassin's bullets.*

In 1921, as Mexico faced the beginning of its fifth century of bloodshed and tragedy, peace came at last. The *Mestizos*, now close to 90% of the population, were finally in charge of their own destiny. From this distillation of 400 years of torture and torment, they emerged as *one* people. Seldom had history been so

---

*We've assassinated a few in growing up in the States, too: Lincoln, Garfield, McKinley, Huey Long, Martin Luther King and the two Kennedy brothers . . .

cruel in the making of a *nationality*. Never, to paraphrase Winston Churchill, had so many taken advantage of so few.

So don't confuse the Mexican with the Spaniard, the Cuban or the South American. He's a Latin all his own:

And proudly so . . .

"Muy Macho" — A Way of Life

"Muy Macho!" is a phrase you hear often in Mexico, in Baja. It doesn't mean simply *"very much a man"*. It means many other things — especially, the Mexican personality that has come out of this past. Americans, from a woman-dominated society, rarely understand. *No comprenden.*

"El Machismo" is a rite of masculinity. It typifies many of the traits the gringo likes — and sometimes dislikes — in the Mexican male.

Our Macho-minded neighbor is romantic, with a raunchy flair. He is often boastful, playing a game. His jests, his bravado, his impulsive, fierce pride are often to prove his manhood.

He is earthy, sensuous. Sex is a sort of badge, a decoration. Perhaps that is why the Mexican fights the bull with more abandon than the Spaniard. Why he drives so recklessly. Why he faces life so fatalistically. Death is to be taunted. When he offers you a drink, don't refuse.

Crimes of passion and revenge are still in evidence. A cuckoo in the nest calls for a bullet in the head. Hers, too. No wonder Mexico once held the highest murder rate in the world.

"Macho" also is the name for a large banana, symbolically masculine. Avocados dangle alongside. The Mexican reads sex into almost everything. But, after all, didn't Freud?

Love Potions and Aphrodisiacs

Aphrodisiacs, love potions and cures for early impotency are naturally a part of the scene. Baja's own Damiana — a liqueur made from an indigenous wild plant — is one historic aphrodisiac.*

Magic and mysticism, rite and recipes handed down from *shamans, guamas* and witch-doctors of the old Indian tribes are still as popular in Mexico as Astrology is in the United States. Today's education resists this, of course, but Baja and the remote regions keep it in a fascinating, half-amused perspective.

The Aztec side of the fiery-blooded fusion and heritage still has its subtle, barely perceptible influences. There is always a precedent for almost any custom or ritual you choose.

"House in Mexico", Carleton Beals' book, insists that the Tehuantepec Indian girls bow to a belief that marriage is more likely if a bride brings a couple of kids to the wedding. So the young girls of the tribe have obliging relationships at an early, semi-tropical age.

Boyde de Mente in "Bachelor's Mexico" indicates that the San Geronimo males, in earlier times, had a similar disinterest in the virgin as a bride. So the mother might send her daughter around to a trusted male friend of the family, or in desperation, even beseech the local priest to oblige.

Virgins of the earlier civilizations were prized by the priests for various religious rites and rights. The twenty Moctezuma maidens sent to Cortés were a heart-warming gift. A young warrior to be honored with sacrifice was given not one, but four, young damsels to share his final weeks. What a way to go . . .

The Spanish *Gachupin* estate owner reserved "first night" rights (or *jus primae noctis,* as other Latins say), with all the girls of his domain. The traditional Mexican song, "La Borrachita", is the lament of a *señorita* who must leave her boy friend to fulfill her sexual obligations to her master.**

---

*Incidentally, don't believe all you hear about "Spanish Fly" as an aphrodisiac. It is neither Spanish, nor a fly. It is a beetle, golden green (in Baja, it grows about a quarter-inch long.) Mexico has outlawed the product, although natives still make their own crude version.

**Cortés had a land grant of 25,000 square miles, including 100,000 Indians. Think of all the "first night" privileges he gave up just to go on and discover Baja.

Pass Your Customs at the Border

But before you get smug about all this, gringo, better check back on the charming little customs that have come out of America's past:

New England's young couples in pioneer days shared a bed in the "bundling" custom, the most fun you could have with your clothes on.

The Mormons, brave men, practiced polygamy.

Plantation owners, down South, raised mulatto children as a cash crop, along with the cotton.

And need we point out our Yankee inventiveness with the commune, "love-in" and suburban wife-swapping "key" games of current times . . . ?

Perhaps it is pertinent to observe a basic difference in the two cultures which has affected our lives in another way.

In Mexico, the conquistadores and the *Gachupines* had two goals: 1) the Indian was to be made a slave, to work the mines, build the missions, farm the land and 2) interbreeding was encouraged from the start.

In United States, the explorers and early settlers had different goals: 1) get rid of the Indian and get his land and 2) import the Negro as the slave.

Reflect a bit on these points and you begin to see how — and why — both the Mexican and the American of today often have opposing viewpoints.

The other differences, gringo-inspired, call for a belated rectification specifically on our part. Care to try?

We're witnessing now a new nation, a new people in a tremendous burst of progress. Actually, it didn't get underway until 1921, fifty years ago. And our "good neighbor" policy so far has given them far more problems than solutions.

THERE IT IS: BAJA!

The future of Mexico couldn't be more exciting. You can help. But, remember: if he hates your guts, he has plenty of reasons.

The Mexicano! Power to him! "Muy Macho!"

Mike McMahan

AMFIBBIN': WHO NEEDS A RETRIEVER?

Mike doesn't need one of Walter's Labrador retrievers to fetch his shoot when he takes this six-wheeled amphib vehicle duck hunting south of Mexicali (near San Felipe). On the edge of Sea of Cortez, one might try fishing in it.

Sea of Cortez:

"Trampa Pescado
Propia de Dios"

3. *Genesis of a Peninsula*
What a Fish Trap!
800 Varieties, Including Whales
Surf Fishing's My Favorite
21 Varieties in a Single Catch
Maybe a 105-Pounder in the Surf?
How the Natives Do It

Whoever called it *"Trampa Pescado Propia de Dios"* invented the right description for the Gulf of California, that beautiful sea between the Mexico mainland and the Baja Peninsula.

"God's Own Fish Trap" . . .

You see, geologists have an intriguing theory that, once upon a time when the Earth was young and didn't have so many ecological problems, here is one of the places ol' Mother broke apart at the seams.

Eons ago — maybe like 4,000,000 years — there was a tremendous upheaval as the hot Earth was told the Almighty equivalent of "Cool It!" and hell cracked loose. The volcanos spewed, the earthquakes rocked and the hurricanes hurled their waters as the molten mass of inner earth seeped up.

THERE IT IS: BAJA!

Then, cooling off, the land masses began to shift about. Slowly, down Baja way, there was a split. The end of the Mexico mainland was cracked open a bit and spread apart. Then, more and more — maybe an inch or so a year — until it is now, eons later, 150 miles distant in some places. "Continental drift", they call it.

The waters of the Pacific rushed in to make a new ocean in between. A new Gulf. So: The Gulf of California.

And Baja, once a part of the mainland, became a peninsula.

What a Fish Trap

Look at the Map. Not necessarily my map. Look at any map of the world. Notice how the Eastern edge of Baja once might have fitted, point and bay, directly into the western edge of the Mexican mainland?

It's the same way, some geologists contend, that Africa and South America once were joined, for the "edges" fit before the continental drift.

Also: the top of the Gulf, near Yuma, Arizona, in the United States, is approximately on the San Andreas Fault Line, mother of earthquakes in Upper California.

You can trace that San Andreas "crack" right on down from San Francisco. Here is where the San Francisco earthquake of 1906* occurred. And there's been many a minor earthquake along the line since.

I well recall one shattering quake in the '40s that shook the Imperial Valley down to its last head of lettuce. It shifted the earth so much you could *see* the path of the fault line. Where it crossed a main highway there was a scar for many months thereafter, even though the crack itself was patched over: the highway had suddenly shifted over two feet to the left, then continued. It was a sobering experience to drive over it.

But, undoubtedly, that one was not as bad as the 1906 one, where a California highway near Point Reyes was jogged over 22 feet!

*Excuse me, San Franciscans refer to it as a "fire". San Franciscans never, never say "earthquake".

800 Varieties — Including the Whales

But whatever the divine intentions, or the geologist's theories about the creation of this new gulf — a warm-water paradise year 'round — it brings an indescribable jubilation to today's fishermen.

The warm waters of the Pacific rushed in and the peninsula made a perfect "gate" for the trap.

Every kind of fish — plus the mammals — that found their way from the Pacific into this new gulf came exploring its many wonders. The current that carried Hoei-Sin (remember him?) probably helped too. Most of 'em liked the balmy temperatures of the surface waters — or they could choose the cool, cool, depths at the bottom where the San Andreas split went down *two miles deep.* (This just happens to be twice the depth of any lake *anywhere* in the world.)

More than 850 species have now been classified in the Gulf of California. There may be even more. Level on level they find their favorite depths (and for cafeteria they have only to swim up to the floor above). Biggest, of course, are the whales who swim in around the Cape from the Pacific and half-way up the Gulf for their own smorgasbord.

It has been pointed out by geologists and ichthyologists that the whole cycle of the Gulf's fish life is aided and abetted by the fact that the Colorado River has, for thousands of years, been emptying its silt and nutrient riches from the watershed of the American Rocky Mountains. Here are the phosphates, nitrates, organic materials to feed the bacteria that feed the plankton that feed the insects and lower forms of marine life that feed, in turn, the graduating larger sizes of fish. All these riches are unending resources for centuries to come. "Vitamins" for future fish, as it were.

It's a fish trap unequaled in all the world.

So you don't have to lie about your fishing exploits here. Even if you break a rod, there's a bigger fish waiting if only you'll tie the line to your big toe.

"Trampa Pescado Propia de Dios."

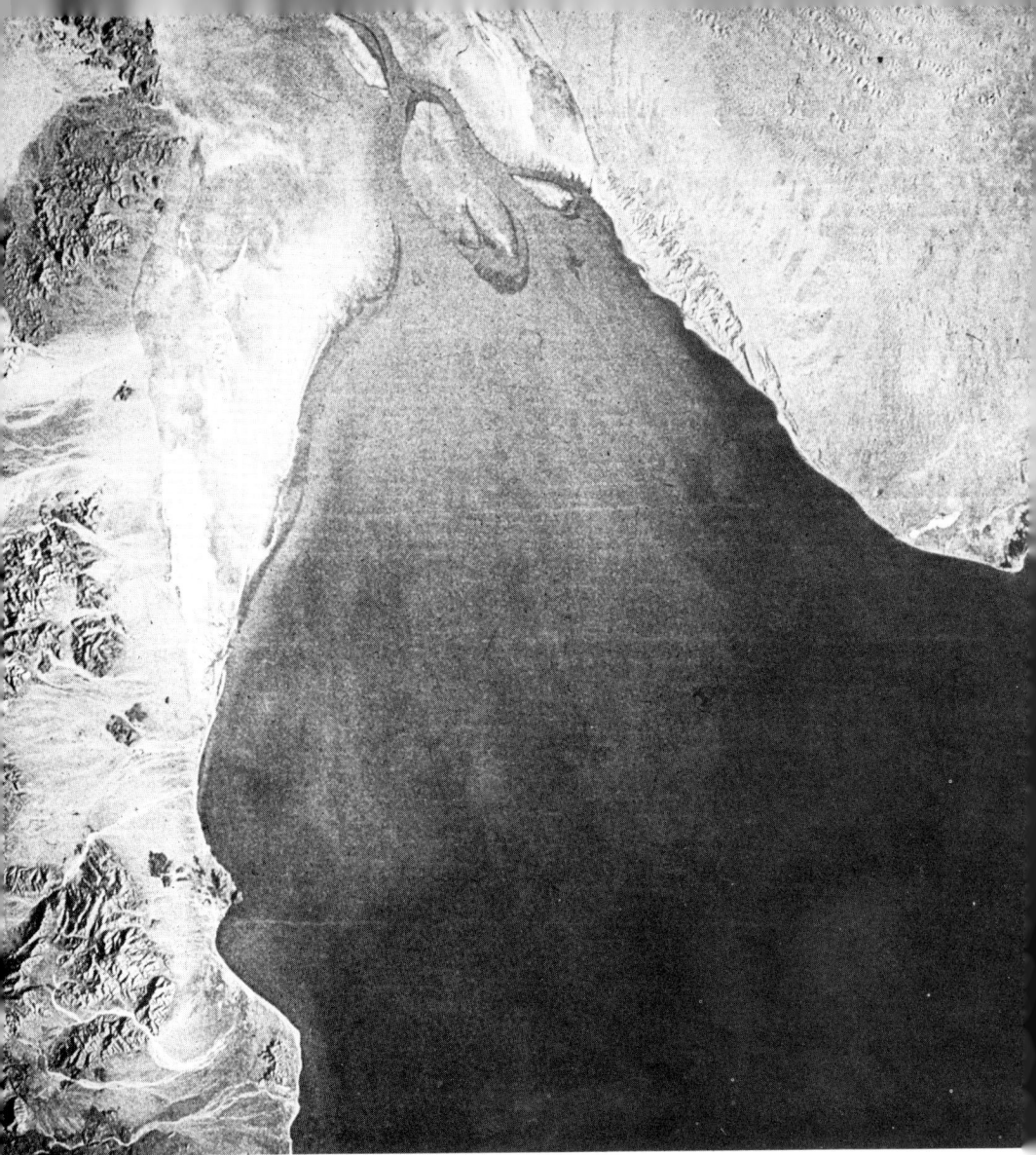

NASA

FEEDING NUTRIENTS TO THE SEA OF CORTEZ

From the NASA satellite's camera position 95 miles above the earth, we can see the mouth of the Colorado River as it flows into the Sea of Cortez. For many centuries, rich minerals and nutrients have been carried down the river from the U.S. Rockies and deposited in the upper part of the Gulf. The larger of the two islands at the mouth of the river is Montague Island, with the smaller Gore Island on the right. San Felipe is located just below Punta El Machorro, the sharp rocky point which juts out into the Gulf near the lower left portion of the photo. As this remarkable photograph shows so clearly, the water becomes deeper as the distance from the mouth of the river increases. Between Punta El Machorro and Roca Consag, soundings indicate depths of 10 to 15 fathoms, with the bottom generally consisting of mud.

— So anything you can do as a fisherman to relieve this overcrowded situation will be appreciated.*

Surf Fishing's My Favorite

I've been fishing in many waters since I was big enough as a Hoosier kid to hang my rod in the Kankakee River.

Fresh or salt water, boat or shore, swordfish or perch, Royal Coachman fly or bent pin. I've done 'em all and loved 'em all.

But surf fishing is my favorite. For sure, this is the most exhilarating — and certainly the most sporting way to catch fish. It's a certain test of patience and persistence like no other fishing. I like it!

And my five favorite spots around Baja's surf shore would be:

MIKE'S 5 FAVORITE FISHING SPOTS:

1) just below San Felipe on the Gulf side at Easter Camp about 160 miles south of the Mexicali border entrance.

2) on Concepción Bay, below Mulegé, another 175 miles farther down the Gulf.

3) below Loreto at Puerto Escondido (Hidden Bay) another 100 miles south of Mulegé.

4) below Hotel Punta Colorada, 90 miles south of La Paz, where I pulled out a 60-pound rooster-fish only last week — as I write this . . .

5) and on the Pacific Side, my vote would go to Santa Rosalillita, a good 275 miles below the Tijuana entrance. Very difficult to reach — but most rewarding.

*Not by me, but by the other fish.

There you'll find, at very low tide, abalones exposed on the rocks. Just pick them up. Then, on the next incoming tide you may even have that rare experience of catching halibut in surf action. (Halibut are only on the Pacific side.)*

21 Varieties in a Single Catch

I suppose it is the wide variety of fish to be caught on a 20-lb. line that intrigues me most about surf fishing. That, and the variety of challenges in playing the fish.

Mike McMahan

At Puerto Escondido our little party caught 21 distinct varieties in just one session. That included a little spear-fishing thrown in by my son, Pat, but it was all right there in one spot. See the picture. It speaks for itself.

Incidentally, Easter Camp can now be reached by normal passenger car as the roads from Mexicali are paved the 125 miles to San Felipe. Easter Camp is another 35 miles on graded (well, sometimes) but unpaved road.

---

*As a matter of fact, halibut are always on "one side" — a "bottom" fish with both eyes on top. Some say the halibut gave Salvador Dali and Virgil Partch the idea for their two-eyed human profiles in art.

But from there the roads are definitely not good and only off-road vehicles can travel easily.

The airplane does it better and faster. Fly to La Paz, then take a taxi plane to Hotel Punta Colorada. Or there's a three-a-week milk-run flight to Mulegé and Loreto. Santa Rosalillita I'll keep for myself, if you don't mind.

What do I like to hook up with? Well:

Corbina (and the related corvina) are first rate sport for the surf fisherman. They're also about 5 pounds of mighty fine eating. Hit a good school of 'em on an incoming tide and they'll strike like stevedores when the docks are loaded.

Cabrilla run up to 40 pounds and can give you a first rate challenge. **Pargo** are in the 30-40 pound range.

Croaker, at up to 10 pounds, can put up a good fight, too.

Roosterfish, up to 60 pounds (best at Punta Colorada). When a school of these are chasing sardines into shore — and they suddenly grab your jig — they just keep coming on. *Qué Bueno!*

There are many more. Depends on the time of year and where you are.

Such fighting gamefish as skipjack, giant yellowtail, garopa, triggerfish, toros and sierra are available year 'round. Bill-fishing is best during Spring and Summer. (But see my chart . . . page 64.)

Maybe a 105-pounder in the Surf?

My friend, Donn Roberts, proved you can pull in a 105-pounder from the surf at San Felipe. It was early morning and the tide was coming in when he made his first cast. Action! The reel moaned in the morning air like a drunken bugler. This was no five-pound corvina . . .

But Donn wouldn't let go. Back and forth he played the fighter. Up on the sand, back in the surf, Donn was screaming like a Guaycura Indian with a bobcat on his back.

For an hour the battle went on. Walter — my brother — and I kept cheering him on from the sidelines with more advice than any good angler cares to take. Finally, the fish was docile enough to follow Donn's line closer to shore. But we had no gaff. Walter had a bright idea: he splashed his way through the surf, stuffed his fist through one gill and pulled the fish up on dry land.

Ray Haller

It was a 105 pound totuava! And we offer as evidence, gentlemen of the jury, the photograph of Donn and Walter (right) and the Trophy — Exhibit B, above.

Who could resist skin diving in water like this? It's difficult, even in color, to portray the beauty of these sparkling waters. This is Puerto Balandra, near La Paz.

Francisco Arámburo, Jr.

Gil Powell

Sea Bass often run several times the size of the fishermen in the Sea of Cortez, where some 850 varieties of fish await discovery by happy anglers and skin divers. This one was brought ashore at Rancho Buena Vista.

NASA

THE CENTER SECTION OF THE GULF

This remarkable photograph, taken at a height of 95 miles from Gemini 5, reveals a portion of Baja California, the Gulf of California, and a portion of the mainland of Mexico at the lower right. At the upper left corner, the Pacific Ocean is almost obscured by the cloud cover, although some of the Pacific shoreline can be seen. Isla Angel de la Guardia is the large island near the peninsula in the upper half of the photo, while Isla Tiburon is adjacent to the mainland at the center. Note the irrigated fields at the bottom right corner; these are west of Hermosillo and northwest of Guaymas. They rival our own Imperial Valley in productivity. Many of the smaller islands of the "midriff" can also be seen; since all of the islands tend to restrict the tidal flow to and from the upper gulf, water currents here are fast and treacherous for small boats much of the time.

Incidentally, Walter says not to try that fist-through-the-gills bit with anything but a totuava. Some fish have razor-sharp gills!

Surf fishing. That's *my* sport — even when I only stand on the sidelines and cheer — and make the photo to prove it!

Donn was using half a shrimp for bait. You can use clams too if you like, but I'm inclined to favor a bright and flashy metal lure, a "spoofer" or a "hoodwink" or the good home-made variety.

Mike McMahan

SURF-FISHING FOR ROOSTERFISH

Walter McMahan and his expert surf-fishing friends haul in their roosterfish. This was near Punta Colorada on the Gulf where the surf sport is superior. Average weight of this morning's haul: 47 pounds. Average playing time: 16 minutes.

Walter, who has been tying flies since before he was able to button* his own, makes a corker out of beer can openers. He calls it an "8-way" and he can twist the metal fins any way he likes to make them flash through the waters and lure the challenge of the strike.

*That was before zippers. Walter's older than I am, you see.

Mike's Fishing Chart

SIZE	LOCATION	SEASON*	HOW TO CATCH
YELLOWTAIL			
5' - 80 lb	Deep water, outer reefs, clear water only. Gulf and Pacific waters.	October thru May — Gulf May thru October — Pacific	Troll with lures or live bait, or surf cast with lures.
CABRILLA			
3½' - 125 lb	Shallow water, rock piles, reefs, entire Gulf.	All Year.	Troll with lures or bait; surf cast with lures.
CORVINA			
30" - 35 lb	Shallow water, rocky or sandy bottom. Near shoreline. Gulf only.	February thru June	Surf cast with jigs or lures; troll near shore with jigs, lures, or dead bait. If birds are working on bait fish driven to surface by Corvina, fish where birds are diving for bait.
CROAKER			
24" - 10 lb	Shallow water sand bottom. Pacific side.	All Year.	Dead bait, surf cast or troll with jig or dead bait.
DOLPHIN FISH			
6' - 85 lb	Primarily deep water but some have been caught from shore. Middle and lower Gulf.	December thru June — Gulf June thru September — Pacific	Troll with bait or cast if school is around boat.
GROUPER			
4½'- 200 lb	Deep water close to shore or rock piles, underwater reefs. Entire Gulf.	All Year. Best in Spring, early Summer.	Dead bait, trolling for smaller groups, deep trolling at level of submerged reefs.
MARLIN — BLUE, BLACK OR STRIPED			
13½'-700 lb	Deep open water. Middle and lower Gulf.	All Year.	Troll with flying fish, jig or mullet.
ROOSTERFISH**			
5' - 75 lb	Shallow water. Middle and lower Gulf.	November thru June.	Live bait, troll, surf cast with jig.
SAILFISH			
7' - 150 lb	Deep open water, outer reefs. Gulf.	May thru October.	Troll with bait or jig.
SIERRA MACKEREL			
3' - 20 lb	Shallow water reefs. Entire Gulf.	All Year.	Live bait. Troll, surf cast from shore.
SKIPJACK & YELLOWFIN TUNA			
5' - 280 lb	Deep water, sounds, outer reefs.	May thru October.	Troll with jig.
TOTUAVA			
6' - 250 lb	Reefs, close to shore, most shallow waters of the extreme upper Gulf area.	March thru June. in Northern Gulf.	Troll or cast from shore with jig or dead bait.

*Season indicates time of year each variety is most plentiful.
**Roosterfish not considered edible.

So You Want The Big Ones?

But maybe you'd rather sit your big, fat duff on a boat and use your beer opener to pierce another can of brew.

Okay, it's a cinch. The Captain can steer the boat, the Mate can bait your hook and you can catch a quarter-ton of these, just between beers, on a good week-end.

Yellowtail, a favorite target for Californians from their own coast line and all the way 'round Baja, shoot like torpedos up the Gulf, too. It's a tough job getting them close enough for surf fishing, but the 30-40 pounders make a real sport of it when you hook one up on a boat. At Concepción Bay, we've seen 'em so thick around the boat you could almost walk on 'em.

Tuna, the yellowfin variety, are less plentiful these days, as the commercial fishermen raid the Gulf and the Pacific shores and leave all too few for the private anglers. For the most part, forget 'em on your target list. Get a can of Chicken of the Sea — the **albacore**, best of the five kinds of tuna — at your corner grocery. Or get Walter to give you a can of his own private label, sealed with a Jalapeño pepper inside.*

You want bigger fish? **Marlin? Sailfish?** A 300-lb. **sea bass?** Maybe a delicious mahi-mahi or **dolphin fish** (not to be confused with the playful mammals called **dolphins** or **porpoises**). And the **totuava**, the fish Donn caught, which is unique to the Sea of Cortez and a spot or two off Japan.

Mount a Marlin On Your Wall

Most tourists want to prove their prowess as fishermen with a marlin or sailfish as a trophy. You can have it mounted on your wall and have a photo made that does wonders as a conversation starter. (It's bound to make all your friends hate you!)

La Paz, Cabo San Lucas, Mazatlán and Acapulco all have resorts that make it easier than the tricks that the safaris contrive to get you a tiger skin.

---

*We give these out at Christmas to our good customers at McMahan Brothers Desk Company. You get an extra Jalapeño in yours if you haven't paid your bill.

Aeronaves de Mexico

MARLIN AT THE MOMENT HE HAD BEEN GAFFED

Even the finest action photographs seldom capture the deep emotional impact every angler feels with his first marlin. The fighting spirit of this great game fish must be experienced to be completely believed and appreciated. It's hard work too, but the aching muscles soon recover and the memory of a great catch will last a lifetime.

One of these blue or black marlin brutes can weigh a half ton and it's no mean feat for the captain, the first mate and the crew to help you land him and still make you think you did it. And whether you did or not — it's still a thrill just to be aboard and see these marlin go into action.

Once you hook up, there's a Fourth of July fireworks show. That marlin plays you back and forth, tearing out to break the line, going up in the air like a Harlem Globe-trotter, plunging to the depths as your reel almost spins fire.

You'll stretch every muscle in your gut to play him in, let him run, play him back in again. I tell you it's a hair-raising thrill, from first tug to final gaff.

Near the Tip is best marlin country. I'll never forget one wild stunt my friend Tommy Foster and I pulled on one of our early trips down to land's end.

We had only a 12-foot boat mounted on top of our jeep, with a 10-horse outboard to power it. At Cabo San Lucas, we launched it and set out to see the sea where the blue Pacific waters lapped into the edge of the Gulf.

Trolling along with a 60-pound line and a dead mackerel for bait, we hooked up with this handsome, big swordfish beauty. He went zing. He plunged. We reeled in just a little. Up he came and — pow! — straight into the air to see if we were still around.

Then off he went again, pulling our 12-foot boat like a toy. We held on for dear, sweet life. Down again. Up! Then he turned, racing for shore. Fine! Just the way we wanted to go . . .

Whooaaaa! He slowed down. Reel him in, Tom! Hold it! He's off again! The blue Pacific now was calling him. Him. Not us.

And this time he didn't stop.* The boat bounced over the waves. Our decision came fast: we cut the line . . .

---

*He wouldn't even wait for a picture. But note the photo of the two sailfish we caught the next day. I wouldn't lie to you.

Mike McMahan

Mortified? Not us. We were lucky to get back to dry land. And we learned a special appreciation for that Japanese kid who was out to cross the Pacific in a rowboat. With that marlin he'd have made it in record time.

Marlin are great. Sailfish are beautiful. You don't have to lie. Anything you ever say you caught in the Sea of Cortéz I'll believe.

Even snook. Or the Loch Ness monster.

I believe it. It's all there: greatest fishing in the world!

How the Natives Do It

Natives have their own tricks for fishing.

Suppose you take a certain cactus, mash the stems and throw it in the water. Pretty soon the fish float up to the surface — stunned — and you just pick 'em up. The cactus that is poison to the fish isn't poison to human beings. So — fish dinner.

CREEPING CACTUS ON THE VIZCAINO DESERT

Cal Karr

The Pitahaya Agria is common throughout the peninsula; it is one of the plants used for stunning fish. The fruit (right) was a favorite food of the Indians, and is still popular with today's inhabitants. The sharp points can be knocked off with a stick; 'till then, handle the fruit with care.

The natives on the mainland have been using the trick in the bays and lagoons of the Sea of Cortéz since before it got that name. On the peninsula, the Indians and later the modern Mexicans, especially around San Ignacio Lagoon, have found it a useful piece of ingenuity.

Hook-and-line fishing was apparently unknown in the southern end of the peninsula, but early explorers found some Indians in the northern part using hooks made of turtle shells or deer horns or from the thorn of the Viznaga cactus (which has a natural hook on it).

The lazier ones preferred their fish wholesale and found two cacti that would do the job. *Garumbullo* and the *Pitahaya agria* are the two cactus varieties — and medical research has since confirmed their chemical fish-poisoning properties.

The *palo de la flecha,* a tree with branches so straight the early Indians used them for spears and arrows, also has the same power over fish. But it is less favored as a poison here because it can be very dangerous to human eyes. Natives caution you: Don't sleep under a *palo de la flecha* tree — your eyes may get a very serious irritation.

But natives talk little about their tricks in fish-stunning. And I shouldn't, either. And neither should you. It's illegal, nowadays.

Guess who got the big one? Walter's wife, Phyllis.

Tijuana:

World's Busiest
Border Crossing

4. *Gambling Mecca of the '20s*
The New Era, the New Lures
"La Mordida" — the Bite
The Horse Nuts
Adrenalin for Gambler's Blood
Olé! The Bull Fights!
Supermarketing for Inland

Baja's peninsula is 810 miles long. That's about 200 miles longer than Italy's. And twice as long as Florida's. Although its width varies, Baja averages about 70 miles wide.

The peninsula hangs down from the U.S. mainland, hinged on its two main cities, Tijuana and Mexicali.

Tijuana is the biggest in Baja — 370,000 and growing like a weed. Mexicali is about 350,000. (These were 1974 estimates.)

Ensenada, where Robert Louis Stevenson once lived and wrote much of "Treasure Island" as he looked out at *Todos Santos*, is third in size. Guess it at 135,000.

Census figures in Mexico are never too accurate. In rural sections, the census reportedly counts the number of windows in a house or hut, then figures 5 kids per window. It's not a bad system and it simply shows the true Mexican has a fertile mind, too.

La Paz, where Cortés first landed, has about 45,000 as it lazes into the Seventies. Most of the rest of Baja towns are only village size as you can see from my map.

But Tijuana is different, for sure. Today it is the busiest border crossing in the whole ubiquitous world. Some half million *turistas* swarm across there on a busy week-end. And there are at least 15-million crossings a year, we'd estimate.

Gambling and shopping are two big lures. The *mercados* are fine for San Diego housewives who want to drive the 17 miles.

Restaurants have a fair-to-spicy reputation. Caesar's Salad was created there.

Modern boutiques and Mexican handcraft shops thrive for the tourists with their bargain "free zone" prices on name merchandise from Paris to Hong Kong.

Mariachi music and the *cantina* bars fill the night with sound and strolling troubadours wend their way your way.

But Tijuana is a shade self-conscious with it all, trying to live down the squalid, bordertown reputation of the '40s and '50s. And live up to its fame and glory of the '20s as the biggest gambling center of the West.

Gambling Mecca of the Gay '20s

Back in 1915, the Mexican government legalized gambling. Tijuana had a population then of less than 1,000 but bold American entrepreneurs went to work. They built a magnificent casino and race track at *Agua Caliente* (appropriate for gamblers: translate *hot water*), in the outskirts of Tijuana.

Gamblers came from all over the world.

Hollywood stars — back when there was real tinsel behind the tinsel and Uncle Sam's income tax was only a minor nuisance to them — flocked there to be seen along with the rich and social western figures of the day. The service was gold, the dinner prices began at $50.00 a plate and champagne flowed like a California oil gusher.

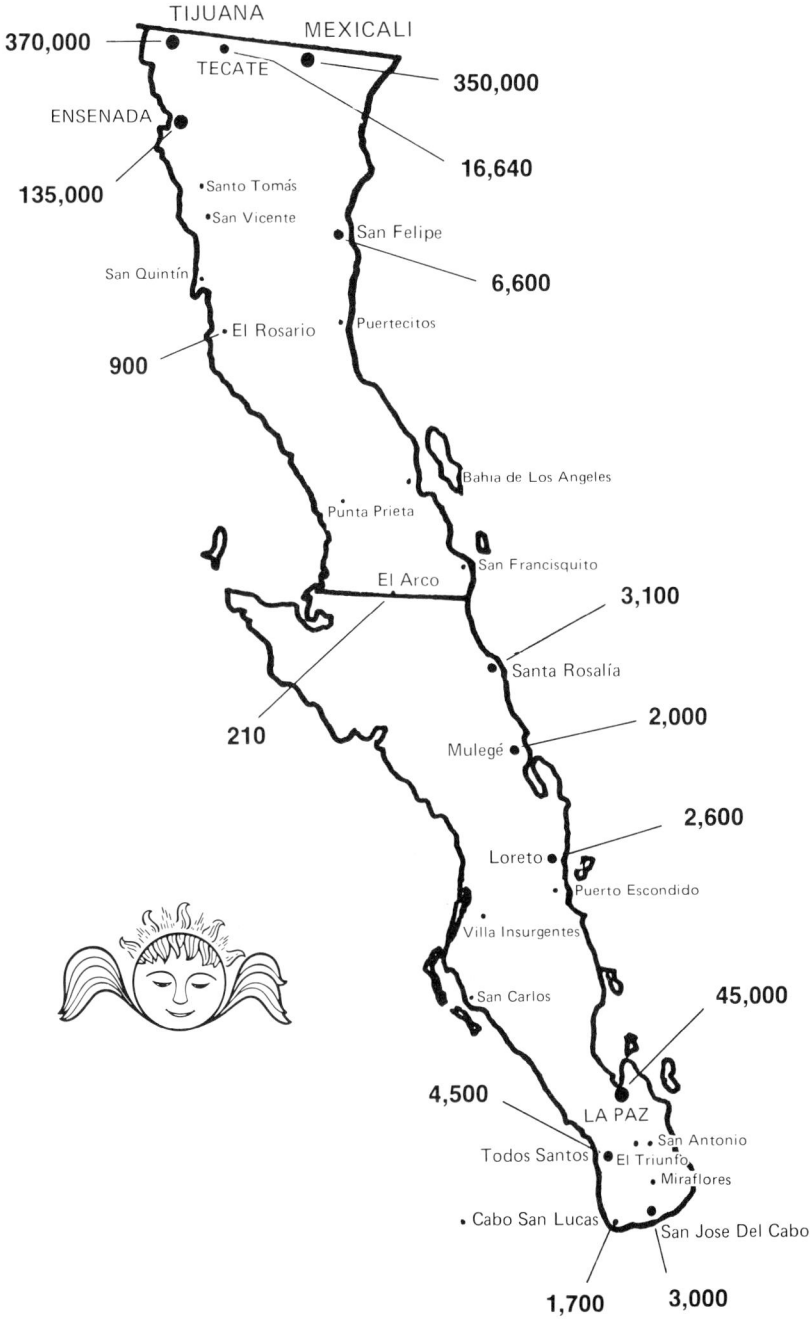

Union Tribune Library, San Diego, Calif.

WHISKEY, 15 CENTS A GLASS — TIJUANA, CIRCA 1924

Riding in the open touring cars of the '20's did dry one out, and Baja had bargains for every visitor. The driver of the truck at left, which appears to be loaded with 5 gallon water bottles, must have needed only a few minutes while double-parked to satisfy his thirst.

Charlie Chaplin came down in his Locomobile.

Tom Mix, grandpa's favorite Western hero, was an honorary field judge at the races.

Mary Miles Minter was there — scandalously pretty, for sure. John Barrymore. Babe Ruth.

Jack Dempsey, then heavyweight champ, was an honorary starter at the races — and later became one of the backers of a big hotel and gambling emporium at Ensenada.

The '20s were roaring. Jazz. Flappers. Bobbed hair. And Booze. Especially Booze.

Prohibition had come to the States so there was extra reason for the thirsty to come to Baja. One Kentucky distillery — Waterfill & Frazier — moved its famous name to Mexico so good whiskey and bad, legal and illegal, was flowing freely — on both sides of the border. Rum runners put an extra 100 gallon tank on their cars to haul it north.*

*Some old-time customs inspectors at the border still "rock" your car to see if it sloshes.

Agua Caliente's races took on international caliber. In 1930 — the start of the depression — they staged the $100,000 A.C. handicap. The thoroughbreds of Kentucky and the East came here. From Australia on the month-long boat trip came the great Phar Lap to prove again his reputation.

But, mysteriously, the "down under" race champion was to die before the big race. Poisoned? Who would say? Horsemen still whisper strange theories.

And legalized gambling was to meet a similar fate. Again, strange theories. The depression of the '30s had come. Nevada had legalized gambling in the United States — and Las Vegas, almost as close to Los Angeles as Tijuana, would vie for the same gambling dollars. Coincidentally, Santa Anita race track opened in Los Angeles in 1934.

In 1935, the Mexican government stopped the gambling. Could it be that certain influential money interests in Nevada were dabbling in Mexican politics? Of course not. That was like the legend of the Amazon woman of Baja and her Golden Bra. Not true.

Even the sailors with Cortés knew that titillating dream didn't wear a bra. She wore golden bracelets.

The New Era, The New Lures

The casino closed. Down the hill, it still stands in dark and saddened splendor, musty, forgotten. On a spring night you can still hear the clicks of the little white ball whirring around the wheel, bouncing in suspense. Or maybe it's the crickets.

Las Vegas won. Tijuana was doomed to years of poverty as it searched for a new way to entice tourists.

Dempsey would rather you'd not mention Ensenada for that monumental enterprise still stands, an emptied dream. The windows are shattered, the cob-webs spread from moldy room to moldy, empty room.

Only the race-track was to survive, a shadow of its early greatness. The names, the plaques, the racing colors of the thoroughbred greats of another generation squinted amidst the dust at the fickle forgetfulness of man.

But the gambling finally bloomed in a new — and very legal — guise. No roulette. No poker. No baccarat for Hollywood stars in tuxedo glory. But racing horses, the "Foreign Book" bookmakers, dog races and jai-alai, all with pari-mutuel frenzy for the new American tourists in sweaty sport clothes.

Across the border below San Diego, the *turistas* charge. One lure: that $98,000 pay-off on Caliente's "fabulous 5-10" two-dollar bet. All the man had to do to win it — once upon a time — was to be the only bettor to pick winners 5 through 10 on the racing card.

World's Busiest Border Crossing

Tijuana is now, as we said, the busiest border crossing in the world. No passport, no visa is necessary — unless you stay more than 72 hours or go beyond the border towns. U.S. driver's licenses are recognized. No smallpox vaccination is required. The U.S. Customs return crossing is very easy — unless you're trying to smuggle too much merchandise or a cache of marijuana or a "wetback" laborer.

Tijuana is getting to be a big, booming city, bigger than ever. Much of the sordid shoddiness of the '40s and '50s is now paved or glossed over.

Tijuana happens to have the highest standard of living in Baja, and, like Mexico City or Caracas, this means the constant attraction of more and more Indians and the poor from the distant, poorer regions. Until they get a job: more shanties.

Fewer than 10% of TJ's 370,000 permanent population were actually born there.

What attracts those hinterlanders to Tijuana? Well, 98 factories flourish. The word is that Tijuana now offers the highest minimum wage in the entire country. And the boom also keeps the building industry and the peso up. The peso (12½ for the American dollar) is more solid than our American buck and has kept its stability for more than 20 years now.

My son Pat took this photograph of a modern wrought-iron shop in Tijuana. This progressive community now has approximately 100 local factories producing a wide variety of products.

Remember, Mexico has the most stable government in all Latin America.

"La Mordida" — The Bite

Tourists need to know about "La Mordida." This is the common Mexican practice of "The Bite" or, bluntly, bribery and graft. Smuggling is a "way of life", the Los Angeles Times concludes, in estimating the situation below the border and in South America. The Times suggests that the volume of illegal traffic into Mexico may be $5,000,000 a year.

"At virtually every customs post in Mexico, be it seaport, airport or border crossing," the Times opines, "contraband is as common as conversation.

"In Mexico, three factors combine to make smuggling an attractive calling: High protective tariffs on most luxury commodities. *Malinchismo* or snobbism, which creates a demand for imported goods. Skimpy salaries that make many customs inspectors susceptible to the bribe.

"Fifty pesos ($4.00) can blind an inspector to almost any item the traveler can carry. A thousand pesos ($80.00) can work miracles."

So: Dutch cheeses, Spanish hams, English cigarettes, Swiss watches, German cameras, and many other items are brought in without the tariffs. A French wine that might sell for $2.00 in the U.S. would, with tariff, cost $9.00 in Mexico. Illegally, the *contrabandista* can offer it for $3.00 and make a profit.

Los Angeles officials report that TV sets and business machines thefted there often "disappear" across the border and have no chance for recovery.

This works a hardship on the honest Mexican importer, of course. And it is a dangerous game for any American to play. Remember you are in somebody else's country and don't get funny with the law — certainly not with the U.S. Customs on your return trip.

Mexican justice works slowly and in strange ways. Don't expect even "La Mordida" to get you out if you get in too far.

In some ways, Tijuana police work with the wisdom of Solomon. For a traffic parking infraction, they are apt to remove your license plate and hold it for legal ransom.

And if a long-haired American hippie crosses the border, they may simply give him a good, close hair-cut — not too neat, necessarily — before they turn him loose back at the border line. Effective! — A short cut to justice, you might say.

The Horse Nuts

Now that you've been cautioned on "La Mordida", let's talk about some of the more attractive aspects of Tijuana. At least to the various segments of the regular habitués.

It is estimated that there is a "hard core" of 100,000 horse race nuts in Southern California who trek across the border from one to six times a week to bet the ponies.

Caliente's special charm for the inveterate bettor is that it also offers the "Foreign Book" off-track bookmakers who'll take your bets on all the major American tracks, from Pimlico to Golden Gate. And "Future Book" odds against future sports events from the Kentucky Derby to the Super Bowl. Morning-line odds and fairly quick race results and pay-offs speed the action through the electronic miracle of Racing Form's wire service from all these tracks.

And here Agua Caliente has an advantage over Las Vegas: there's no 10% U.S. Federal Tax on bookmaker bets. To the estimated 3% of all gamblers who actually do make a living betting on the races, that 10% is the difference between profit and loss.

Never mind Las Vegas' other charms.

Adrenalin for the Gambler's Blood

"They're off at Aqueduct!" ... "Results coming in from

New Orleans" . . . "Closing now at Rockingham — get your bets in!" . . . "Here's the winner of the second race at Santa Anita" . . .

The loudspeaker re-creates the ecstasy and suspense, minute by minute, and it's adrenalin for the blood of the horse gambler. Some 56 races may be reported on a single day, sufficient chances to test the mathematics, luck and pocket-book of even the most maniacal of players.*

Aeronaves de Mexico

Not enough gambling for you, yet? Then try the *jai-alai* games at the *Frontón Palacio* on Thursday, Friday, and Saturday nights.

Jai-alai is the very exciting Basque sport (translation: *"Merry Fiesta"*) that derives from handball. Some seven centuries ago they began playing handball with sticks, later tried it with racquets. Three centuries ago they developed today's *cesta*, a long curving basket-like "mitt" that fastens to the player's hand, catches the *pelota* and whips and spins it over beyond the opponent's reach.

---
*Like my brother, Harry. He'll bet on anything. He'll even bet you that you can make money betting on the races. (Hmmmm . . . that's a good bet!)

It's a fast game. Sharp players. Sharp spectator sport.

You can bet on it . . . for Baja has its pari-mutuels there, too, for any *turistas* who have the mistaken idea they might be taking some of their gringo dollars back across the border.

Olé! The Bull Fights!

But there are no pari-mutuels at the bull fights. There wouldn't be much point, since the bull always loses. And some good charity winds up with bull steaks that night.

However, we trust you are not a stupid Anglo-Saxon with preconceived ideas that bull-fighting is a blood-thirsty sport. It is a competition, perhaps a sacrificial ritual. And, correctly, the Latin says *corrida*, "the running of the bulls," not "bull fight."

Perhaps you should go . . . with a Latin aficionado so you may learn to appreciate the grace and style and finesse of the *matador*, the ritual of the *picador*, the whole ceremonial pomp and pageantry of the ring.

It is Life!

Life is that brave bull rushing at us, trying to bruise us, crush our bones, rip our guts out and spill our blood upon these sands. How close can we get to Life? Can we tempt its dangers with insouciant flair? Can we trick Life by hiding behind that red, red cape and stepping aside at the last split-second?

Always, in our hearts, we know the story is the same: Life must come to an end . . . a meeting all too short. We are the matadors. The question is: how do we meet Life? Bravely? Dangerously? With a scornful smile and a flourish? Do we make our encounter with Life an art?

If you have never been to a bull-fight, go. Play the role. And it would be well to have an *aficionado* at your elbow to sit beside you, to whisper in your ear and to shout — as you find yourself shouting:

"Olé!"

Tijuana has two rings for the bull-fights. Some of the best matadors in Mexico and in Spain — even the great Manolete himself — have come here, on a May to October Sunday afternoon, to encounter Life . . . *

Shop the World in an Afternoon

Many a *turista* comes to Tijuana with never a thought of gambling or the bull-fights, though. They come to shop.

What to buy? Hong Kong jade, Burma ivory, Japanese cameras and electronics, French lalique, Italian figurines, British Wedgewood . . .

Christian Dior is in the boutiques. And Pringle and Jaeger. And Pucci and Gucci. Name the international brand, they have it, all tidied up with the price neatly shaved.

Don't overlook the *uniquely Mexican,* though. No, not the gaudy, claptrap souvenirs, but search for the good Mexican handcraft specialties that now abound:

>Modern silver jewelry from Taxco.
>Black lava pottery from Oaxaca.
>Copperware from Michoacan.
>Colorful rugs and *sarapes* from Salinas.
>Glazed ceramics from Guadalajara.
>Onyx stone sculptures from Baja's own mines.

Or, search the side streets and find the custom craft shops. To your own design they will make wrought iron, lamps of glass and metal, hand-tooled leathers, or tile and ceramic specialties.

Still want a souvenir? How about one of those colorful *piñata* toys that hang from the ceiling of some of the shops? In festive paper donkeys and owls and rabbits there are hidden a world of little gifts and surprises for the child's birthday party — or Christmas fun.

---

*There's "do-it-yourself" bullfighting at Cortijo San José, incidentally, if you have the inclination — and the guts to spare . . .

Pat McMahan

Maybe a souvenir for yourself, just one? You're bound to pass a Tijuana street photographer who has painted his burro with zebra stripes. And you can adorn yourself with a sombrero and a gay sarape for the momentous occasion.

Especially after a day of gambling, there's nothing like a snapshot of you, with that still brave smile on your face, that sarape over your shoulder, a Mexican *caballero* sombrero tilted rakishly on your head — and you on your Mexican ass.

Olé!

Supermarketing for the Interior

The chances are you won't be going on to the interior. Only 1% of Tijuana's tourists look deeper into Baja. If you're the 99%, go home. Don't waste my time.

But if you're in the 1%, I'm talking to you. You'll be stocking up some provisions at one of the good supermarkets in Tijuana (or in Mexicali, if you're heading down the Gulf side, to the East).

Baja's canned goods include many equal or superior to the Stateside equivalents. You can trust these brand names:

> *Envases* cans excellent peaches.
> *Clemente Jacques* does a fine job with mangoes and other native tropical fruits.
> *Cal-Mex* stuffs green peppers, intriguingly, with baby shrimp and tuna.
> *Santa Fe* is a good name for dried fruits.

There are several brands of good tuna and sardines, packed in near-by Ensenada, where the catches are freshest. Ensenada is also the "yellowtail capital of the world." If your liking is octopus or turtle, these are canned in Baja, too. And peppers. Lots of peppers. La Paz cans great pimientoes.

Some markets offer such delicacies as hearts-of-palm and wild honey that has come from the mountain caves of Baja. Recommended.

Canned bacon is good for a long trip into the hot interior.

Stop by the bakery and pick up some of the Mexican breads for the trip, too. You'll especially like the crunchy little dinner rolls, *bolillos,* and there are a lot of *pan dulce* sweets to catch your eye and water your mouth.

Take along the Mexicali Beer (remember, water is scarce . . .) Bohemia and Carta Blanca Beers are excellent, too, provided they come from the original, mainland *cereceria* in Monterrey. Coca-Cola is okay — they have just built a 7-million-gallon-a-day water purification plant in TJ.

HEADING FOR PUERTO ESCONDIDO: 1952   Mike McMahan

If you like rye whiskey, try Waterfill's — from Juarez. It's the best guard against snake-bite I've found. Isla Santa Catalina has a breed of rattlesnakes that have no rattles — and, scout's honor: Be Prepared!

Now, it is estimated that 15% to 30% of all visitors to Mexico come down with some form of intestinal disorder. Don't worry. Just stop by the *botica* (drug store) and be sure you have a supply of Entero-Vioformo* or some other relief from dysentery (a malady also called "Moctezuma's Revenge" or the "Mexican Two-Step"). Not that you have germs to fear so much, but a change of food and water in travel anywhere can give you a pants-down up-set.

And we don't want to stop every five minutes waiting for you. We're heading for the interior . . .

Let's get to the heart of Baja.

*This product has been banned in Japan, due to side effects from over-usage. Still okay in small quantities. Or you might try the new Furoxone which is guaranteed to "cement" relations abroad. Recommended dosage: Take 1 pill every 4 hours, whether you are standing up or still sitting down.

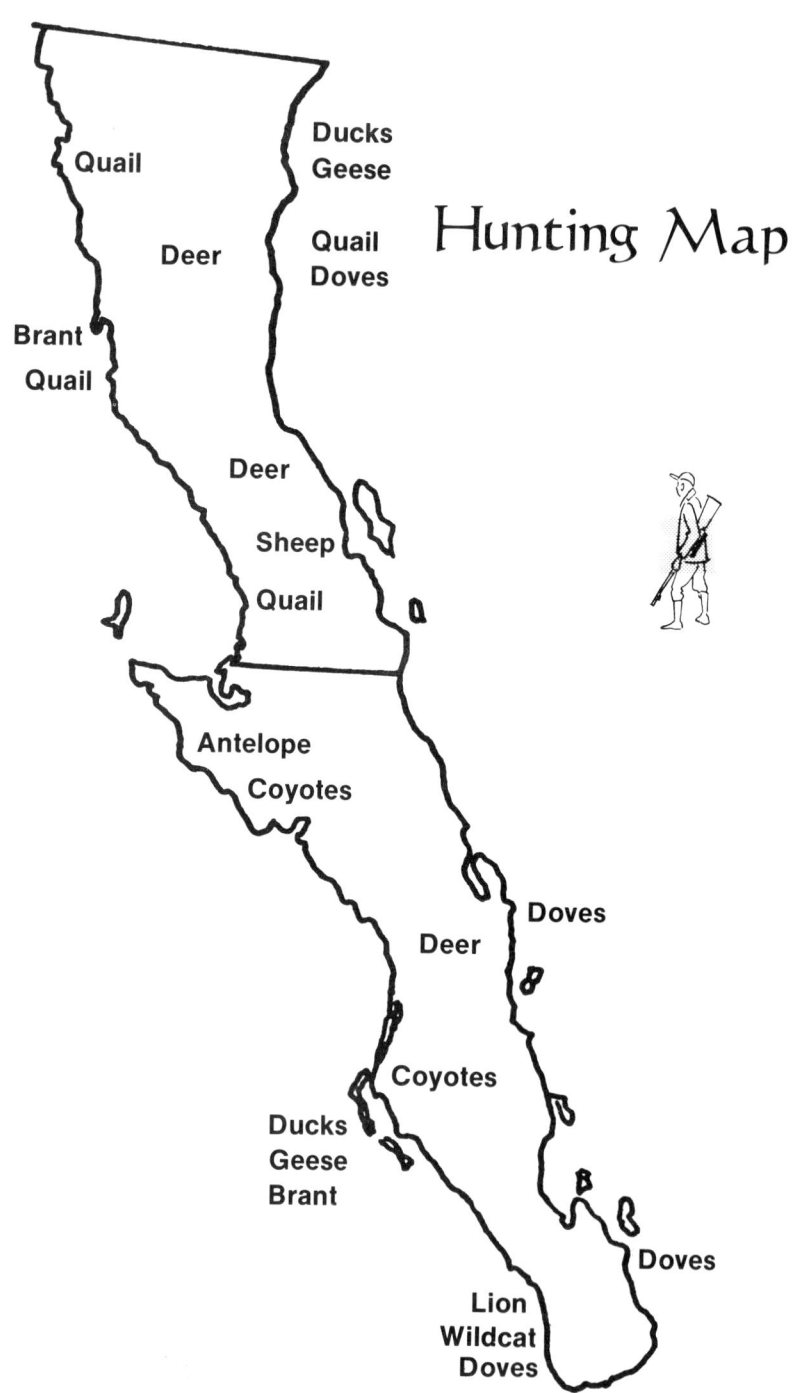

Baja by Camper Truck:

The Rugged Center Section

5.
The Three Parts of Baja
The Desert's a Killer, for Sure
Four-Wheel Drive: "La Burrita"
Special Check List for Baja
My Friend, the Fayuquero
Time in Baja Doesn't Run, It Strolls
Death in the Desert

Now, keep in mind there are three sections to Baja:

1. The border towns and the upper third with paved roads and modern facilities.

2. The center section, especially the primitive desert region with *no roads* or very bad roads.* Volcanic in origin.

3. The lower third — the "Tip" — with its tropic splendor and luxury resorts.

The Baja terrain, in general, has always been described as the worst possible land to travel over.

The missionaries and the first explorers spoke of Baja distances in *time* rather than *miles.* And the hours or days referred to foot travel over the faint Indian trails.

*At least this is how it was until the new road was opened in 1974.

Even the importation of mules and burros did not speed up travel time significantly because there were few places in this land where a beast carrying a burden could travel much faster than a man on foot.

The ox-cart, familiar in the rest of Mexico, never quite made it in Baja. Only when this century turned over on new motorized wheels were trails widened enough to permit the travel of anything but mules and men in single file.

Sea travel supplied the early attempts to establish the mines and colonies. The nearest suitable bay or beach on either side of the narrow peninsula made the water routes simpler and better than roads. (Why else were most cities built on water access locations?) Roads could wait for a later day.

The ships came from La Paz or from the mainland of Mexico. There were ports of call on the West or Pacific Coast at Santo Domingo, Miller's Landing and Santa Catarina. On the East or Gulf Coast: El Barril, Bahia de Los Angeles, and Puerto de Calamajué.

The First Roads Begin to Emerge

Only short roads to the mines were needed. But as some of these were abandoned and new mining ventures were tried farther inland, some roads began to show two tracks for a wheeled vehicle rather than the one of the early Indian trails.

But it was not until the mid-1920s, they tell me, that it was possible to drive from Rosario to San Ignacio. And that was at great risk to your springs and your mechanical ability.*

In 1925, expeditions from the Automobile Club of Southern California toured the length of the peninsula, mapping the road and erecting signs of a sort. This opened the center section for the first time to adventurous American tourists. Mostly hunters and fishermen.

Other mapping expeditions have been undertaken in recent years (and we began our own in the 1940s). But very little was actually done to change the condition of the so-called roads. The

*And your aching back.

PARKING AREA FOR START OF ANNUAL RACE — ENSENADA TO LA PAZ

It's called the "Most Brutal Road Test in the World" and this is an accurate description of an unbelievably difficult endurance run. Although the race begins and ends on paved roads, it also includes the worst of Baja's ruts and gullies in the rugged central portion of the peninsula. Many eager competitors start the race but few finish it; every serious contender risks death from equipment failure or errors in judgment. Only those who have traveled Baja's unpaved tracks in the desert can fully appreciate the hazards; the racer who wins must combine superb equipment with personal stamina, skill, and lots of luck.

government simply had no money to spend for construction or upkeep. Only the brightening prospects of today's Baja now makes it possible.

But that's where the action is, if you're an explorer at heart.

Let's just be certain you're not a foolish one.

Here and there you may read a story by some novice explorer of Baja, telling of all the death-defying adventures he encountered and slightly over-emphasizing these very mishaps. Most were caused by sheer stupidity, lack of planning and the neglect of primary precautions.

Win Muldrow

Above: When racers must slow down, they are often enveloped in their own cloud of dust — but this is the least of their worries. Below: The Baja 500 takes its toll too; the race is shorter but the risks and the terrain are just as terrible. This racer turned over; note angle of front wheels behind the "totaled out" hood remnant.

Win Muldrow

The Desert's a Killer, for Sure

Make no mistake, the Baja desert can kill you. In cold, cold blood. Be warned, be certain you have the proper respect for what you're getting into: "The Land That God Forgot".

The North third of Baja is amply modern and comfortable by comparison. The South third has places of tropic wonder and luxury.

But the middle third: Look out! This is rugged country. You'll have to be a special person to appreciate its own quiet, often awesome satisfactions.

There are no half-way measures about any desert. One either falls in love with it at first sight, or one is repelled. A few visitors take one look and shake their heads in bafflement. They cannot understand how anyone could enjoy living in such a desolate, sun-seared place with its mysterious silence.

Others feel their aches and pains disappear in the clean dry air and respond to the ever-changing colors of the extraordinary desert scenery. At night, the stars are hung up like lures on fishing poles. And moonlight makes it a super-natural dream of lights and shadows.*

The casual traveler who visits the desert during the winter season is likely to think of what he is escaping at home rather than of what he finds there. He may call January days "springlike," and insists the warm days in March and April are "summertime." When flowers do bloom and birds chatter their winter conversation pieces, the stranger expresses enthusiasm for the desert's "perpetual summer." He even asks the desert dweller if he finds the lack of seasons monotonous.

Of course not. Winter is winter and summer is summer, even in the desert. The desert spring and the desert autumn may seem a little short. The change from winter to summer and back again is much quicker and more abrupt than in other climes. But anyone who has lived the year's full cycle in the desert knows well enough the vast differences that occur in the desert's seasons.

---

*It's a paradox in this space age, but Baja's clear skies make it ideal for watching the various satellites orbiting the earth. Any night: see at least two or three.

The Last Unexploited American Desert

Over the past thirty years, almost all of America's desert areas have been explored, exploited, and occasionally populated. Human footprints now are found on the most remote animal trails. Jeep tracks continue where roads end. And communities mushroom wherever any excuse encourages them. However much the desert dweller and the "pioneer" deplore this surge of civilization, nothing they say is going to stop it.

Nevertheless, the stranger who comes to the desert, any American desert, in search of solitude today may find it already crowded out. The only way he can really "get away from it all" is to go to another country. South. South to Baja, the last desert area still unexploited on the North American continent. Care to risk it?

Water — fresh drinking water — is invariably your biggest problem. Without it, you're a goner. You may go for days without food, but not without water. And you have to plan to bring it with you, because oases are rarer than the thirsty man would like. Even the occasional ranch you find may be abandoned — for lack of water.

Remember, Baja's *annual rainfall* is less than 10 inches — but that may mean 2 inches in La Paz, 30 inches in the nearby mountains — and *nothing* in the desert.

Patton's army, training in the Southern California desert during World War II discovered the same thing. Working on a grant, eight PhDs conducted experiments for four years. Their conclusion: Man cannot live anywhere without water. Any desert prospector could have told them that in ten seconds. So you better believe it.

Can you "live off the land"?

Yes, if you have water to drink. (But it's also thoughtful if you have brought salt, cooking oil and flour ...)* On the shoreline there are plenty of fish for the catching. Plus clams and lobsters and other sea foods which require only spearing or grabbing.

---
*And whiskey, in case of snake bite.

Ray Haller

"La Burrita" number 1 featured a special body, custom-built by Mike and Walter; the truck was a basic Jeep. The rocks are typical of the area near Canipolé, which is south of Bahía Concepción.

And, if you have a gun, there is some small game: especially the desert rabbits and the quail and dove.

Thorny brambles may have berries (but be cautious, the Squatberry is as laxative as its nickname suggests . . .)

So the desert begins. The Vizcaíno Desert surrounds that hook on the Pacific side, half way down the peninsula, and extends almost to the Gulf on the other side.

Four-Wheel Drive: "La Burrita"

From El Rosario, some miles below Ensenada on the West side and from San Felipe or thereabouts on the Gulf side, a normal passenger car just should not try to cope with the roads.

We have had four types of power vehicles in our years of exploring Baja to its Tip. "La Burrita" — little burro — has always been the name. And all have been 4WD.

"La Burrita I" was a basic Willys Jeep for power and we built a special body on it to hold our gear — plus plenty of water, plenty of gasoline.

Ray Haller — We made some changes when we built "La Burrita" segunda. More power from the gears in this Dodge Power Wagon, plus more road clearance and larger tires. The cabinet work on both sides accommodated our gear and many storage areas were built to fit the items precisely. The awning gave us lots of shade.

"La Burrita II" was a Dodge Power Wagon which gave us a little more power on the rough roads, a little more speed on the paved highways from Los Angeles down to Tijuana. A little less aching back.

"La Burrita III" was a Ford four-wheel drive truck, with again a special body which took into account some of the things we had learned on the earlier vehicles.

Now we have "La Burrita IV", an International truck, ¾ ton with a special body. Look at the photographs of the "Burritas" and you can see how we adapted.

You'll find the basic reminders on camping equipment on any Auto Club or other check list. But we now add a few more, based on our own foolhardy experiences in Baja:

Special Check List for Baja

A good jack. (The best you can get, not just the usual bumper jack that comes with the car. A good 5 ton — or even 12 ton — hydraulic jack makes the work easier.) And, need we remind you, a complete tool kit and a tow chain or tow rope.

Sherilyn Mentes

No matter where you camp in Baja California, it's pleasant to stop early and enjoy your surroundings. This is a shaded campsite right on the beach at El Coyote, on the western shoreline of Bahía Concepción.

Below: This is Puerto Chileno Bay, at the tip of the peninsula. Fishing is excellent, and all types of water sports are more fun — and usually more productive — in the incredibly clear water found here.

Francisco Arámburo, Jr.

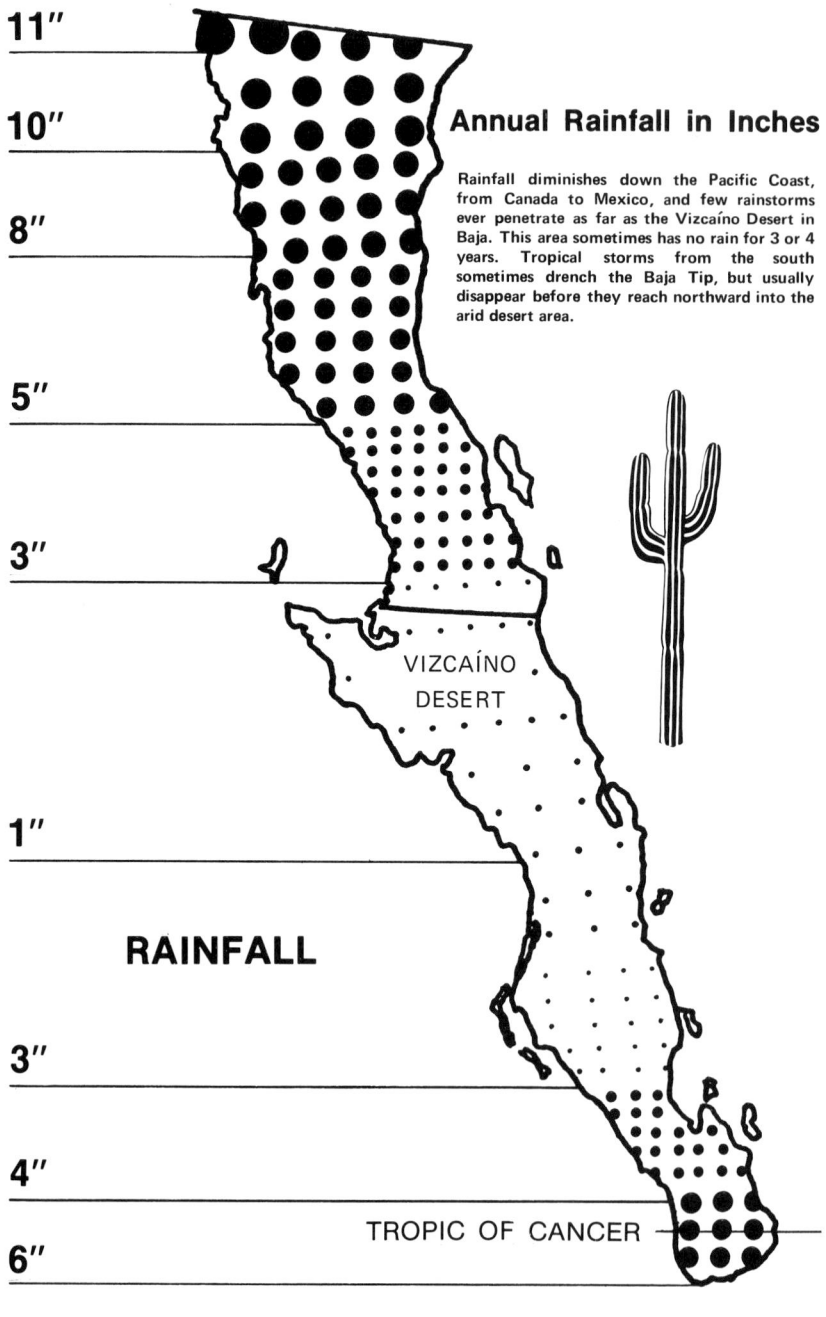

Above: Our third "La Burrita" was a Ford truck. Better highway speed than the Dodge plus a quiet transfer case. More comfortable cab, on or off the highway. Note extra storage space on the roof. Below: "La Burrita" number 4 is an International truck, 3/4 ton with highly functional body. It has virtually all the comforts of home built right in. Over a period of twenty years, each new camper has included new features we learned to appreciate from experience, during thousands of miles of primitive travel below the border.

Two spare tires, at least. Plus **tube-patching kit**. We strongly recommend the old-fashioned tire with inner tubes rather than the current "tubeless" — because on sandy roads you may want to let down the air pressure to 10 or 12 pounds.

Spark-plug tire inflator (for when the roads get good again). Plus a hand pump, in case that inflator decides — like everything else — not to work.

Tire gauge, tire irons.

Battery-jumper cables.

Plus: spare fuel pump, coil, points, condenser, belts, five quarts engine oil, spark plugs, wiring, hoses and clamps, fuses, cup grease, an extra set of keys and a chamois for straining the native gasoline.* Take 'em whether you consider yourself a mechanic or not, because almost any Mexican who drives these roads *is*. He has to be to survive with some of the old, battered trucks that make these backbush routes.

My Friend, The Fayuquero

This Mexican truck driver — or *fayuquero* — is your friend. You cannot — repeat, *cannot* — trust the road information you get from the villages or ranchos or even many of the older maps and guides that are printed. But the truck drivers who push their ancient vehicles over this part of the country have to know every problem and short-cut between here and there.

Fayuquero seems to have meant, originally, a "peddler on horseback" but here in Baja the word has changed with the times to indicate these itinerant merchandisers who overload their trucks with staples and supplies, canned goods and clothing, barrels of gasoline and used furniture, and set out for the remote villages and many of the isolated ranchos. Home base may be La Paz or Ensenada or even Tijuana.

The traveling merchant sells what he can and buys or trades for local items to overload that return trip, too. Country cheeses, wild herbs, crude sugar, hot peppers, dates, dried fish, cows and cowhides, goats and goat skins.

*And some more whiskey. Just in case you run into another snake.

He has to know the country. You can depend on his road information. He also is apt to supply much of the regional news and gossip while he's at it — a traveling newspaper, as it were. Sometimes he carries messages — or even mail — between remote points. Occasionally, he may take a passenger. Most of all, he's a pretty good mechanic, a genius at improvisation in keeping any old motor ticking along.

One such character I met on a steep, stony stretch south of El Mármol. He was having fuel pump trouble. I started to offer some suggestions, but then I saw he had his own native adaptation of the same principle.

He had wrapped wire around the arm of the fuel pump that touched the camshaft so it would work the diaphragm a little harder. It had worked before, he said, and sure enough, pretty soon he had it working again.

Another Good Reason for Inner Tubes

Another time, in the rocky stretch above Socorro, I stopped for a stalled truck beside the road. (It's not simply the "rule of the road" to stop and offer help — you often learn something you hadn't expected . . .)

This *fayuquero* had been operating in second gear *only*. Sure, he had the other gears — look! There they were in that box, over there! What's more, he had *no* generator, *no* water pump, *no* fan, and only one headlight.*

As he puttered with the transmission, there was little I could do but listen. And it was well worth it. He showed me how to get water out of a "barrel" catcus. I had always thought that was just a legend but he proved it could be done and we'll pass the story along to you in a later chapter.

"Gracias!" I was most grateful. As I left I noticed that, in addition to the other infirmities of the battered truck, one of the tires was completely worn through and the inner tube was bulging out like an overgrown tumor.

Could I offer him a boot for the tire?

---
*General Motors — or Ralph Nader — should hire him as a consultant.

IN BAJA, FLAT TIRES ARE NORMALLY "DO IT YOURSELF" PROJECTS

Be sure you have any special tools needed for the wheels you have. Items shown here are best for split rims. A little soapy water helps during bead breaking and re-assembly; the large special hammer breaks beads loose from the wheels, and special tire irons fit slots in split rim. Spark-plug kit for pumping air is most desirable; used for flats and also re-inflating tires that have been deflated while traveling sandy areas. Large lug wrench provides added leverage; canvas keeps everything out of the dirt. Add plenty of patches and a few boots, and you're ready to handle normal punctures. Handy accessories: two beers. One before, one after.

The *fayuquero* shrugged his shoulders and said, "Ees okay, señor, she runs..."

The *fayuquero* philosophy is simple: never fix anything that doesn't have to be fixed until it has to be fixed.

Time in Baja Doesn't Run, It Strolls

Time, itself, finds its own philosophy in Baja.

Americans say "a clock *runs*" or "time *runs* out". In Mexico, they say a clock *walks*, time *walks*. (*"anda"* from the verb *andar*). It just strolls...

So, learn to slow down to a walk and enjoy your Baja travel more.

On the middle third of the peninsula, the roads being what they aren't, you are wise to hold your day's travel down to 30 or 50 miles, on an average. Even less, if your time permits.

Slow speed over these rough and rocky roads makes it easier on the springs, the tires and your own nerves.

Select a good campsite and stop early, before you're all worn out. Make a comfortable camp. Take the more pleasant, more beautiful sunset hours to do a little hunting or fishing, make a few camera shots or just stroll around and appreciate the weird, desolate beauty of this curiously forbidding land.

If you have come in February, March or April, you may be treated to a wild flower show that will make the contrast spectacular. It is as though Frankenstein's monster had suddenly bought himself a new tie.

Every plant, shrub, cactus seems to have hailed Spring with the wildest collection of blooms you can imagine. There, among some grotesque species of cactus your eyes catch sight of the most unexpectedly beautiful blooms . . . yellow, red, magenta, lavendar, cream or scarlet.

Or notice how the trees strain their way through rocks and sand and raise their own bloomin' flags in victory. And over there's a *cirio* tree with its oddly waving stem asking you to come-hither.

This Baja tree looks like an elephant's trunk and suddenly comes out with bright pink, cream and red blossoms. Another looks like it has sprung from a shrub to hoist its triumphant flower stem on a slender branch.

In this barren land, a tree may be so stunted it looks like a shrub, while the many varieties of cactus often look like trees.

About trees and cactus, more later. But here is the desert — and it can be deadly. So maybe a few pointers for the venturesome camper are more urgent at this time.

Death in the Desert

Water — let me nag you on this point — is more important than food when you go exploring through this desert country of Baja. Baja's biggest problem through the years — to the padres, the colonists, the farmers and the traveler — has been the lack of water.* The rainfall is so low, the temperatures often so high, that water is very scarce. It is essential to carry an adequate supply, and especially in the arid central section.

De-salination of the sea's ample salt water may soon compensate as various projects in this work continue in Baja (as around the world).

But, meantime, take with you plenty of the fresh, unsalted variety.

If your car breaks down, lack of water can be fatal. Now, I don't want to be a fright-peddler, but I've had one or two experiences that have embedded the lesson in my memory.

My boy Pat and I were on one of our trips of desert exploration. It was as recent as July, 1968, and we had just pulled into camp at Villa Mar y Sol, just south of Gonzaga Bay, when we were asked to look at a dead woman in camp.

The desert had taken its toll. Their truck had broken an axle and the man, about 50, and the woman, about 30, had tried to walk the seven miles to this camp.

He had finally stumbled into the camp that afternoon, alone, almost delirious. Three men went out to search for the woman and found her — just a half-mile from camp — crumpled under a bush. Dead. Seven miles later. Dead.

— So one learns to respect the desert.

And water.

---

*Scientists have proved that quail in Baja are not even inclined to mate until after a thunderstorm breaks the desert aridity.

Malarrimo Beach:

Loot for
Beachcombers

6. *Junk Heap for the Pacific*
By Sea, By Air? No . . .
Tough Trek by Desert Road
There It Is: Malarrimo!
Steamer Chairs — and Plane Wrecks
A Chance to Dig History
Aschmann: Early Explorers

If you lust for the loot of the Pacific, Malarrimo Beach may be the most exciting place in all Baja for you. With, nearby, a whale of a sight — the sight of whales, mating . . .

Here at Malarrimo is where the Pacific waters collect and hide their spoils and treasures.

If you're a beachcomber at heart you may find washed up on this beach the wrecks of a dozen ships, a few bottles of Scotch, a hundred wooden sandals drifting over from Asia.

Or tins of food from another war or the pretty, bright blue-green glass balls from a Japanese fisherman's net — or a life jacket that turned out to be a death jacket . . .

Oceanographers call it the end of "The Longest River in the World." For 9,000 miles this branch of the Equatorial Current has moved past the Philippines, upward to Formosa, sweeping by Japan to the Aleutian Islands and Alaska, then down our Pacific Coast, to swirl on this "hook" that juts out, halfway down the peninsula.

Here is where Hoei-Sin, the Buddhist monk and adventurer, may have floated across the broad Pacific to visit, as he wrote in the annals of China in 499 A.D., this land of "Fusang".

And here, too, is where whole colonies of the forebears of our Indians could have floated to short-circuit the generations-long land trek by way of Alaska.

At any rate, whoever came to Baja may not have stayed long. Hoei-Sin may have been forced to go farther south, perhaps to Peru for the return current that carried him back to Asia and the writing of his odyssey.

Any others might have been moved on Eastward Ho. For this is Malarrimo, so named by the later Spaniards:

"Bad to get near . . . " *Mal,* bad; *arrimar,* to get near.

Flotsam and jetsam, the Pacific has made it a wastebasket, a junk heap to hide the guilty evidence of its storms and mishaps. —To the delight of any adventurous beachcomber.

By Sea, By Air? No . . .

We had heard the legends of Malarrimo for many years before we first had the guts to try to get there.

For sure, it's no place for the casual tourist.

By sea, it's a dangerous voyage for small craft and a larger boat can be grounded and pounded to pieces. Halfway down the peninsula, the mouth of Vizcaíno Bay lies aslant the north-south "river current", a trap for the Pacific debris — and any unwary sailor.

By air, the litter on the beach makes treacherous hazards for

LOOT FROM MALARRIMO BEACH... Happy looters (l to r) are: Frank Whipple, Pat McMahan, Monica Whipple, Marie Whipple, Jim Isler, Poncho Whipple, Chuck Potter, Ginger Potter, and Mike McMahan. This is a beachcomber's paradise.

Mike McMahan

Mike McMahan

Above: This was one of our campsites on a trip to Malarrimo Beach; often they're so appealing that we'd really like to stay longer than overnight — so we do. **Below:** We found this old ship hull almost completely buried in the sand at Malarrimo. From the evidence we could put together, it appeared that the ship had burned.

Mike McMahan

landing. The beach itself is an inviting arc almost 15 miles long; but buzz it low in your plane and you will see the problems and debris spread out on the beach below you. The closest air field, even today, is nearly 75 faulty road miles away.

By land was the only way, we decided. The maps then were vague. Roads just weren't. A barren desert and craggy mountain outcrops had fenced the sandy graveyard in.

But we had heard the stories. And we had visited isolated ranches not too far inland where the houses had been built — and oddly furnished — with the wreckage from the ships.

We had to go.

So . . . we went.

Tough Trek by Desert Road

The Vizcaíno Desert is about as mean and fearsome as they come. Cactus and sand and sun and rock. Here and there a scorpion. Certainly, it is the last place in Baja I would recommend for the tenderfoot.

And maybe the first for the explorer.

Even the antelope we once saw there have almost completely deserted it, leaving it to the scrawny jackrabbits who stay only a hippity-hop ahead of the hungry coyotes and the less-than-friendly rattlesnakes.

"La Burrita", our first camper, was stocked for this trip as never before with water and gasoline. On food, we could give a little. After all, we had a recipe for Jackrabbit Jon and on two occasions we had found that fried rattlesnake — liberally flamed with whiskey — could be every bit as tasty as frog's legs.

Malarrimo Beach is actually only 375 miles by air from San Diego (if you have a parachute), but it is 628 miles of meandering road by truck or four-wheel drive vehicle. Don't attempt it in anything else. From El Arco, the mid-point village on the peninsula — halfway from top to bottom, half-way from westside to eastside — there are still 160 miles of uncharted land to travel.

BOTTLES TRACE PACIFIC CURRENTS

Four bottles used for tracing the currents of the Pacific wind up at Malarrimo. These were released by the University of California (Scripps Institute of Oceanography at La Jolla) to check on ocean currents. Malarrimo's "hook" captures an incredible assortment of sea-going items . . . it's a beachcomber's paradise.

By compass, by often unreliable word-of-mouth direction, we headed out. At a dozen key points we had roughed out on our own map, we knew a wrong turn would lead us East to the Sea of Cortez, not West to the Pacific.

The best way, we guessed, was through a canyon with sun-baked sand hills on each side. It was narrow, rocky with only the trace of a slow-going trail.

Slow-going, it was. At least, you met no Detroit-type traffic. The only "traffic fatality", natives say, was a gringo explorer bit to death by a rattler. It seems he was changing a tire . . .

The last 17 miles were slower than a man could walk. Almost a snail's pace.* The road follows a twisting canyon *arroyo seco*, a dry gulch complicated by shifting sand dunes that narrow the going. If the rocks don't get you, the sand does. But we admitted it was worth an occasional stop just to revel in the colors of the canyon walls. Soon, even over the desert sand we began to smell the fresh, salt breeze from the bay.

There It Is: Malarrimo!

We began to pass the first signs of this strange beach fully fifteen miles inland. Perhaps the beach had once come up to here. True, much of this land long ago had once been under water — even as far up as San Diego, geologists say. Had the Pacific kept piling up sand along with the debris to stretch the beach farther into the ocean? Had there been earthquakes and giant tidal waves to add to the land face?

It could have been a tremendous tidal wave from times past that had piled up those massive redwood logs and stumps we had seen so far inland. Or maybe because Malarrimo Beach is edging itself seaward, scholars say, at a rate of an inch a year.

For amateurs, the intrigue of the stories mounted. The salt breeze was keener now.

Then, over a sand dune, we saw it for the first time. Against the setting sun — that come-hither star of every explorer — the evening's fog wisped and rolled and flirted with the beach. And look at that beach!

The prow of an ancient boat — maybe three, four hundred years old? — lay nosing out of the sand, as though trying for one more gasp of air, one more lap of the surf. Over there lay a bright yellow lifejacket battered but certainly of a more modern age. It had been used *once*.

All about: the blue-green glass balls, escaped from float duty on Nippon fishing nets to travel halfway 'round the world. And driftwood from a dozen distant forests.

---

*Almost, but not quite. A snail is officially estimated at .03125 miles per hour. You can crank it up faster than that.

Ray Haller

ANCIENT REDWOOD WINDS UP IN BAJA

This gnarled base of an ancient redwood tree, probably from the Big Sur country near San Francisco, ends up at Malarrimo. Now embedded hundreds of yards above the high tide line, it may have been swept ashore by a Pacific storm of another century. And before this century passes, it may be hidden by the shifting sands.

Amidst all this: tins and tins of army rations.* Candy we found, cigarettes in waterproof containers and foods of all kinds.

And look: a torpedo! Alive or dead we didn't know — and we didn't care to put ourselves to the same question by taking off that handsome brass propellor. (But we did make a photo of it to report to the Coast Guard.)

Steamer Chairs — and a Plane Wreck

Over there, steamer deck chairs and the wreckage of a plane. Sure enough, Malarrimo was not a very safe landing strip. And there were hatch covers by the dozens (today, haul 'em back, varnish 'em up and they'll fetch a hundred dollars as coffee tables at the antique shops).

*Hey, Mac, how about a little Spam? The sailors must have chucked it overboard, can and all, to save time.

Mike McMahan

SPOILS OF THE SEVEN SEAS

Trophies from a day of beachcombing at Malarrimo: Mike & Ray Haller check out the spoils. In the foreground, the boxes show points of origin. The next tide may bring a case of scotch . . . or the wreck and refuse of the Seven Seas.

But that night the hatch covers made the best sort of wind-break for our camp fire on the beach. We decided to try out the corned beef in one of the tins, along with the coffee from another. Good! There was plenty of lifeboat emergency drinking water tins for the coffee, too.

It turned out to be quite a meal. We were living off Malarrimo Beach, even as we explored it.

The next day we tried our luck at fishing. But it was obvious it could never be the fishing wonderland that we had found just across the peninsula in the Sea of Cortez.

The surf is too rough. The water is too shallow. The area itself is simply too inaccessible.

For the explorer, yes. For the beachcomber, yes. For the fisherman, no. You can catch enough for a meal and that's about it.

**MIKE HAULS AN OLD SHIP'S SUPPORT RIB
TO CAMP AT MALARRIMO BEACH**

A Chance to Dig History

So don't come to Malarrimo Beach for the sport of Izaak Walton. Come as a kid — with a pail in your hand — to dig in the sand and see what you can find.

For, beneath this beach are surprises enough. An expedition might well dig history here. If that prow of the ship rests on still an older ship, when did it come and what did it contain? Spanish gold? Pirates' plunder? Hoei-Sin's calling card?

The beach is as wide as a city block and, if it has been extending itself seaward at the rate of a few feet every fifty years, what secrets does it hold beneath it?

No, a metal detector isn't apt to find gold for you. Actually a detector would "ping" itself crazy — and your hopes along with it — unless it had a handy needle that could distinguish between the yellow metal and the basic ones that rust and corrode. For our explorations showed many scraps of steel and iron and brass buried throughout the beach. Engines — steam, diesel and gasoline — that launched many a ship, clutter under the surface, perhaps alongside the belaying pins of an earlier sailing era.

Aschmann's Account of Early Explorers

Homer Aschmann, who wrote a thesis in 1959 on "The Central Desert of Baja California" (University of California Press; now reprinted) offers some fascinating accounts of the early Jesuit explorers at Malarrimo:

"During his exploration of 1751, Father Consag made a detour to look at a sandpit in front of one of the lagoons in this embayment", he writes.

"His Indian companions collected pieces of crockery, including Chinese porcelain and other artifacts of Old World manufacture, and reported that the shore was littered with such material as well as broken ship timbers".

DETAILS OF SHIP'S SUPPORT RIB FOUND BY MIKE

No one knows the age of this support rib from an ancient sailing vessel; it could have come from a Spanish galleon. Note the hand wrought bolts and how the grain of the wood follows the curve of the piece.

Other accounts corroborate the stories of the shipwrecked timbers and provisions to be found on Malarrimo Beach. One reported that the timber of one of the old wrecks, when touched by hand, disintegrated into dust.

Is it possible that, deep underneath the surface, there is some ancient wreck covered by sand that is better preserved?

Indeed, the sands of Malarrimo are ubiquitous, moving slowly but relentlessly. We had suspected this first on the canyon road coming in as we saw the dunes edging over the old tracks as though they wanted to obliterate an intruder. On a later trip they had taken new positions again,* now setting a different obstacle course.

On the beach, the dunes move with the same restlessness. A wreck half buried in the beach today may be completely covered in a few months. Or, stranger still, it may be left high and dry on a pedestal of sand. The wind of the northwesters will soon whip it clean as a statue, a monument, a gravestone in this odd, desolate cemetery.

What treasures have been buried with the dead?

STEELY SKELETON OF THE BAJA IRONWOOD

This is the ironwood tree, Baja's rare hardwood. Its foliage gone, it weathers to steely hardness in desert air. This is one of a dozen such prizes Mike has collected and fashioned into a craggy base for a unique glass-topped coffee table.

*Like a politician in election year.

This photo was taken in Scammons lagoon, territory of Baja California by Ralph White, Jan. 1974. The foreplay of the Bull Gray Whale may last as much as an hour during courtship.

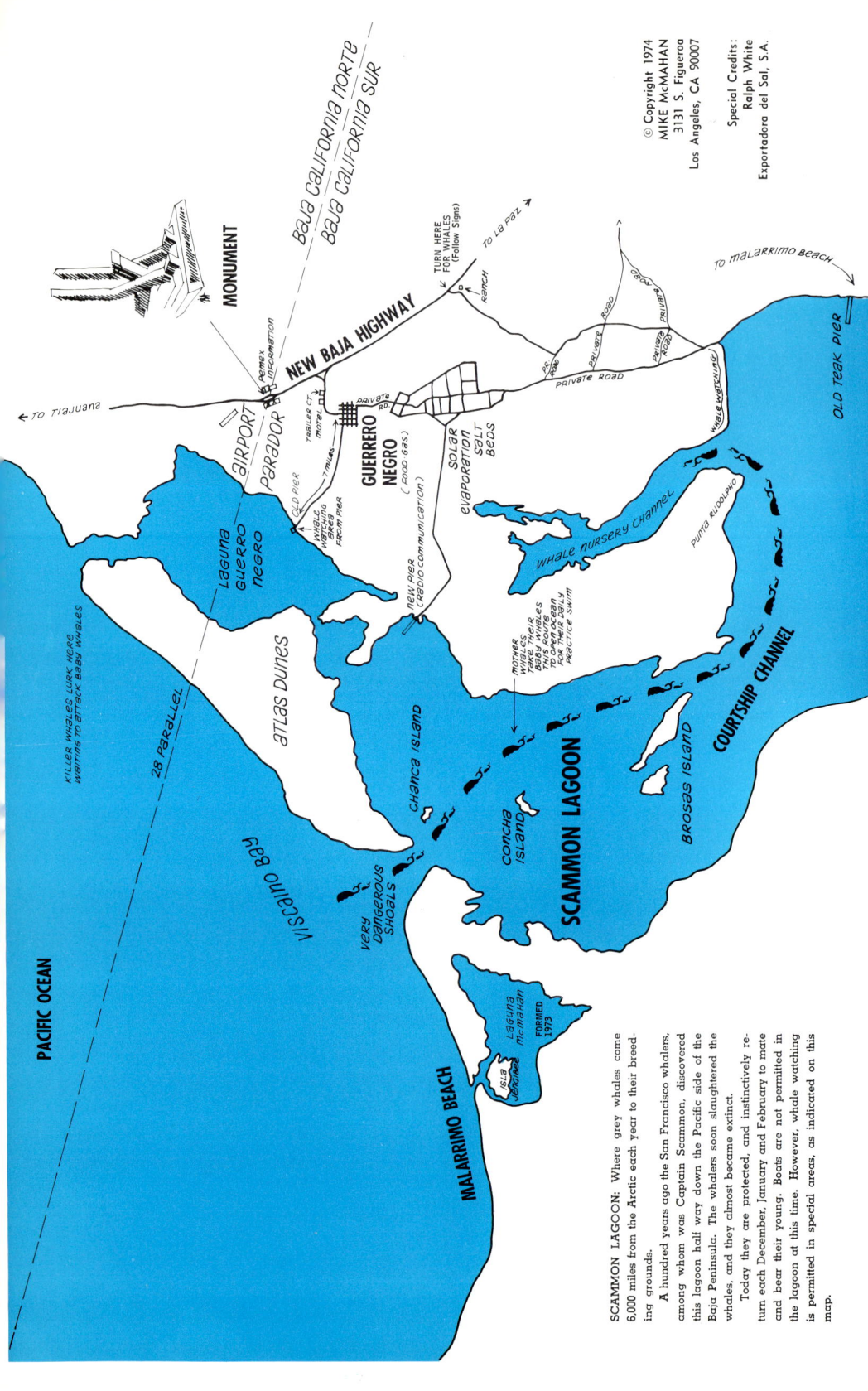

Tale Of A Whale:

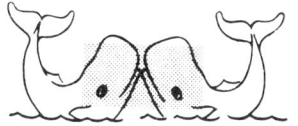 Scammon Lagoon

7. *Where Whales Come to Play*
Sex and the Single Whale
Captain Scammon's Secret
Heartbeat of a Whale
Historic "Kitchen middens"
Sea Shells for Collectors
Steinbeck's "Pearl"— and a Philosophy

In all the central part of Baja, the desert section, there is probably nothing more fascinating to today's explorer than that beachcombing trip to Malarrimo.

Yet ten minutes away is a lagoon that is an easy second for interest.

That ten minutes, however, applies only if you have a helicopter. By road it will take you at least *ten hours* — a full, hard day's driving.

Scammon Lagoon is right next to Malarrimo. On the map. But there's no road, no way to get through, so you have to double back and around, circuitously.

It's worth it.

Plate XXVI.

A NORTHERN WHALING SCENE.

Courtesy of Captain Scammon's granddaughter, Mildred Decker.

Above: Charles M. Scammon was the most famous of the Pacific Coast whaling masters. His spectacular successes while hunting the gray whale brought him almost instant renown in his home port of San Francisco. Most whaling captains would have been delighted to retire with only a fraction of the fame achieved by Scammon, but his remarkable drive also revealed his talents as a good artist, a self-trained naturalist, and an accomplished writer. Louis Agassiz was one of the notable men who greatly admired Scammon's work, and spurred him on to publish his book. Opposite page: Although this illustration from Marine Mammals refers to a northern whaling scene, it also indicates how Scammon Lagoon must have looked at the time when the good Captain unwillingly shared his discovery with the other whaling ships which followed him into the lagoon.

For that's where the whales come to play. And mate. And calve (for whales are mammals like us, not fish).

Captain Scammon was one of the last of the great Pacific whalers back in the days when whale oil was lighting the lamps of the world. And whale meat didn't wind up tinned for cat food as it often does today.*

Those were wild adventurous days, with deadly battles between the crews of the rival square riggers for the 30-ton specimens. A rugged whaling man might just as soon throw his harpoon through a competitor, if he got in the way of one of these big prizes.

Captain Charles M. Scammon died in 1911 at the age of eighty-six. What a character he must have been! The salty old seaman who dominated an era, the most famous of the Pacific whaling masters.

San Francisco was his home port and few men knew the business as he did. He took a scientific approach to the whale and made it a point to know more, always, than his competitors.

He was a self-trained naturalist, a writer and a reasonably good artist. His charts of Baja and its waters are still classics.

Sex and the Single Whale

It was Scammon who searched out and discovered the breeding grounds of the California gray whale in this then remote lagoon off Vizcaíno Bay.

Most whalers and the early coastal packets at that time avoided this seaward stretch of Baja like the plague. The current was treacherous. The winds were strong. The depths uncharted. The mouth of the lagoon too narrow.

The sex drives of whales and men *are* different. Two years may be too long for a sailor to wait, but it's just right for gray whales at the end of their long migration. Perhaps it isn't accurate to say that never has something so large traveled so far to get so

---

*Yes, they still catch whales today to help feed the 27,000,000 cats in the U.S. today. And a few human beings overseas.

HARRY BET IT WAS 6 FEET LONG

In the interests of science — and to win a bet — brother Harry stands beside this trophy of a male whale to prove it is more than six feet long. Mike purchased it from a private collector who insists it once hung as a fertility fetish.

little. But Scammon followed his own instincts and, utilizing the knowledge of whaling for which he became famous, followed some of the largest creatures in the world to this isolated lagoon where the instincts required for the survival of their species were satisfied. The techniques used by Scammon for taking the whales were cruel and devastating, but in common use by the whaling vessels of that period. Scammon was a brilliant executioner of these giant creatures, but he was no conservationist and didn't claim to be.

Captain Scammon's Secret

Of course, when Scammon found the secret of the lagoon for which history now cartographically remembers him, he tried to keep the secret a secret.

But rival whalers kept observing Scammon's ship return to San Francisco with a full cargo of whale oil each time. And all in such a short time, it meant a short trip.

They followed him. They found the secret lagoon.

And the slaughter began. The gray whale was almost exterminated, at sea — as the Indian aborigines had been, on land. The rival ships fought bitterly between themselves for rights to the love nest. And many a cow never lived to return again to calve.

The massacre never was stopped completely until 1937 when conservationists in U.S. and Mexico forced international laws to protect the whales. Even so, by then, the whale oil lamps around the world were flickering out and the whaling ships had long since hung up their old-fashioned harpoons.

Captain Scammon retired to San Francisco and in the 1870s published his observations on whales — and dolphins, seals and sea otters — in "Marine Mammals and the American Whale Fishery." This rare book has recently been reprinted by Manessier Publishing, Riverside, Calif. It includes an extensive new introduction and some of the Captain's own charts of the Lagoon and Baja waters which, for some strange reason, were not included in his original book. If you prefer one of the original copies, printed a hundred years ago, you might find it a good buy at the going price of $500.

— If only Captain Scammon had known what it was going to be worth!

The only "whaling expedition" to enter the Lagoon in recent years has been a scientific exploration party, in 1956, which sailed there with the improbable dream of recording the heartbeat of a whale.

Heartbeat of a Whale

Dr. Paul Dudley White, President Eisenhower's heart consultant, was the one who wanted the cardiogram of the whale's heart. National Geographic Society helped subsidize the venture and an 83-foot diesel craft was provided by Donald W. Douglas of Douglas Aircraft.*

" . . . whereas man's heart is roughly the size of his two fists, the heart of an adult gray whale would overflow a bushel basket and tip the scales at more than 250 pounds," wrote Dr. White, reporting on the expedition. He had spent forty years in studying the hearts of everything from mice to circus elephants; now he wanted a cardiogram on a whale.

"The mouse's heart, we found, beats 500 to 600 times a minute, while an elephant's pulse thumps only 35 to 40 times," he wrote, estimating the whale heartbeat at perhaps fewer than 10 times a minute.

But Scammon Lagoon refused Dr. White an opportunity to confirm or deny. The 20th century harpoon, with nylon-insulated wires trailing from its head to a following radio-transmitting sea-sled, never was to hit its mark. As the little harpoon boat passed a mother whale she thought her calf in danger and slammed a gaping hole in the craft. Another boat was tried, but this time a whale flicked it off with his tail.

Time ran out on the expedition and they quit — (ah, yes — as before them, Cortés and the padres and so many Baja adventurers had quit). And so the heartbeat of the whale was not to be recorded.

Today, these same gray whales have proved they have plenty of heart. From the slaughters of the whalers, they have come back strong. Visitors can go to the whale-watching station in San Diego — at Point Loma — and see some of 8,000 gray whales now in the

---

*A good customer of McMahan Bros. Desk — and kind enough to grant permission to use their notes and chart on the expedition.

Pacific as they parade and spout on the way to their playground in Baja. The peak months are January and February, with minor action in December and March, as the instinct strikes.

Or, better still, come on down to Baja, to the Lagoon, for the incredible excitement. But better come by helicopter — and bring your camera with you.

At Scammon Lagoon . . . near Malarrimo Beach!

Historic "Kitchen Middens"

Below San Quintín, below Vizcaíno Bay — and on two-thirds of the way down the Pacific side of Baja — is Magdalena Bay.

Here the ocean and the Equatorial Current toss a few left-overs of flotsam and jetsam. And the fishing and clamming are remarkable.

The clamming obviously has provided food for centuries and the early aboriginal tribes knew all about it. They lived beside the water and clams were the mainstay of their diet.

Today, traces of their lives are hard to come by — except for remains of their clam shells. They simply tossed them in a heap and the stacks grew and grew. Archaeologists call these mounds "kitchen middens" — refuse heaps where earlier man threw his mollusk shells and animal bones after he had eaten.*

Some "kitchen middens" we have seen in Baja appear to be more than 20 feet in depth. No animal bones. Just clam shells. Generations upon generations of clam eaters.

What happened?

Surmise: The nomadic natives moved down to the shore, ate the largest clams first. The supply of big ones gone, they were forced to eat the smaller ones, on down until the bed was almost exhausted. The tribe then moved on up a few miles to another beach and the cycle started anew at that location. Maybe 15, maybe 20 years later they moved back to the old beach and the

---

*He was lazy. And there were no ecological enthusiasts to make him feel guilty about it.

Ray Haller

MILLIONS OF SHELLS

Above: Until you've actually explored a few of Baja's astonishing kitchen middens, it's difficult to believe that so many shells have been tossed aside by so many natives over such a long period of time. This photo was taken south of Loreto; desert growth now struggles to reclaim the land. **Right:** Because the mixture of old shells and earth doesn't provide much contrast for the camera, it's hard to distinguish the layers of larger and smaller shells shown here. Perhaps you can see the one layer of larger shells near the middle of the cut; this midden located 12 miles south of Santa Rosalía.

"kitchen middens" received another layer of the big ones, then medium, et cetera, et cetera.

Baja is known to have the largest collection of "kitchen middens" in the world but little actual archaeological exploration has been done here. Perhaps much more is to be learned, some day.

So far, they have found few traces of pottery in this area. Maybe pottery wasn't needed.

After all, clams are one thing you can find already packaged in a shell. The shell also doubles for carrying. And again, for the clambake, that shell is a cooking utensil. Finally, it serves itself up on its own shell: a mouth-watering morsel that has brought its own plate to the feast.

Sea Shells — And a Pearl to Remember

Baja's sea shells are some of the most beautiful in the world. Natives gather them for the tourist trade as well as to ship to wholesalers in the States. But why not gather your own?

The tides cast them up on the beach. And what you find for a trophy today you'll probably discard in favor of a more beautiful one tomorrow.

Around the reefs, you can easily find more than a hundred colorful, semi-tropical varieties from the broad Pacific. They come in every shape and size, in stripes and colors and intricate formations to please the artist in your soul. And sounds — sounds of the distant sea as you hold them to your ear — perhaps to remind you of the Sea of Cortez, down Baja way.

The beach south of San Felipe is considered one of the top spots for shell collectors. Although our interests are more towards the good-eating inside rather than the good-looking outside, we often pick up a few intriguing shells at low tide. These come naturally sand-polished in interesting patterns in black and brown. One in every few thousand is a blonde, rare enough to have considerable value.*

*For one-in-a-billion odds: Walter's son, John Michael, found a shell with "JM", his initials, on it. Note the picture across the page.

Mike McMahan

John Michael was thrilled when he found this unusual shell bearing his own initials.

Sea shells may be anywhere around the shoreline of the peninsula. Especially in the clamming spots and the sheltered beaches of a bay inside a larger bay.

Abalone shells, to be made into jewelry, are there on the Pacific side for the hobbyist. Native artisans dabble in this work, too, and you'll find these among the trinkets at the tourist spots. Or from an urchin vendor along the streets who would like to haggle with you a little before you buy.

Pearls? Old timers remember when a pearl from La Paz waters sold for $18,000! — That was in 1908.

But the pearls are no more. Some of the old timers insist that the Japanese poisoned the water so that oysters could no longer thrive in competition. But that seems unlikely as the pearl industry of La Paz was already slacking from the peak finds of the early part of this century.

Actually pearls were a business in La Paz as early as 1540, shortly after Cortés first landed. While searching for gold and silver, pearls might be a conquistador's best friend . . .

But if you find a pearl oyster alive today, don't take it. It's against the law.

Steinbeck's "Pearl" — And A Philosophy

John Steinbeck's "The Pearl" tells the story of how the finding of such a treasure complicates a man's life beyond his own power to control it and enjoy it.

I think of that often as I hear the old-timers tell the story of the $18,000 pearl of 1908. And then I see life as it is lived by the natives of Baja . . . and their ever-present dreams of such a find . . . or that pot of gold in the mission's walls* or maybe the Mexican lottery . . . *El Premio Gordo* — the Fat Prize!

But maybe not all dream the dream the same way.

One day I met an old Mexican beachcomber on the sands near Cabo San Lucas. It was no Malarrimo for treasures, so far as I could see.

"Do you pick up," I asked in my best Spanish, "enough things of value to make a living by this kind of work?"

"Enough, señor. But it is *not work* . . . "

"But did you ever find anything of real value — like maybe a few old gold-pieces washed up on the sand?"

"No, señor. And the hope is that I shall never find anything, as you say, of real value . . . "

---

*We'll tell you about that in Chapter 12.

Mexican Ingenuity:

Tips on Lots
of Things

8. *Tips Around the Campfire*
Tips for the Road
Fishing and Miscellaneous Ingenuity
Dad Had a Trick or Two, Himself
The Point of the Cactus
Ingenuity with Language

In this modern world — you are reminded on a Baja camper trip — there is nothing like an exploration of things primitive to keep our so-called modern values sorted out. And to appreciate the hardships — and the simple joys — of generations past.

In 1910, only 4 Americans out of 10 lived in the city. Now it has risen to 7 out of 10 and, by 1980, the prediction is 9 out of 10.

Nine out of ten, trapped in the city! What a pity!

"Escape to Baja", this is McMahan's solution. And, even amidst some of the comforts we've built into the "Burrita" wagons, I still get a charge out of doing much of our camper truck living in more native ways.

---
*This is the maguey cactus. From its center comes a "milk" that can be fed to babies. Full of vitamins! This juice also can be fermented to make pulque, mescal and tequila. Adult vitamins!

Native ingenuity is always something to appreciate in the study of any primitive or pioneer culture. The aborigines of both American continents discovered, long ago, many of today's useful drugs among the native herbs.

The New England pioneers had enough "Yankee ingenuity" to foretell a parade of our modern inventions.

The Sioux knew how to preserve their buffalo meat in long, lean weather-beaten strips of jerky for the next summer's wars. And how to swallow large hunks of it (with the help of a whack on the back!) so the stomach wouldn't know hunger for days . . .

Necessity, said an observant man named Wycherly, is the Mother of Invention.*

You really need a native instinct for improvisation — along with your check list — to survive in these parts of Baja.

That old *fayuquero* took time to show me the trick for water.

Let's put that down for Tip One:

Tip 1. WATER FROM CACTUS: The "barrel" cactus is just that — a fat bulbous prickly thing, like a watermelon on end with hooked thorns. Cut off the top, then dig down and make a hole about the size of a quart bottle. Now build a fire under the cactus. Soon the sap pours into the hole — presto: "water!" (It'll *do* if your life depends on it.)**

---

*And the desert is an unforgiving father.

**Another method, possibly easier and more efficient, was described by Frederick V. Colville in an article beginning on page 499 of the Smithsonian Annual Report of 1903. Colville was in Sonora, where this method was used by both the Seris and Papagos. Some of the comments are so pertinent for survival in the desert that a number of extracts are quoted here:

"A stranger left alone in a desert would die of thirst, and yet there is water in all deserts, and both the native animals and the native races know how to find it . . .

"Some of the largest cactuses, such as the saguaro . . . the pitahaya . . . are not available as a source of drinking water, for their juice is bitter and nauseating. But the juice of certain species of the genus Echinocactus, notably E. emoryi and E. wislizeni, is sweet and palatable. These cactuses, the Mexican name of which is bisnaga, are known by all natives of the desert region as a potential source of drinking water . . .

(Continued on next page)

But if you run out of water in hot weather, you may not be lucky enough to have that misfortune happen amidst a batch of barrels. A man needs about a gallon of water a day — or maybe a little more — to prevent dehydration.

Tips Around the Campfire

Maybe you are the kind that takes along a butane or gasoline stove when you go camping. Fine. But consider the advantages of campfire cooking. It's cheap, safe and never gets out of order.

It'll keep you warm, you can cook on it and then, after a good campside supper, you can see the *conquistadores* and the padres — and, dimly, maybe an Amazon woman — parading through the smoke of the embers.

Tip 2. PICK UP FIREWOOD: Remember, wood is scarcer in the north part of Baja and in the Vizcaíno Desert. Learn to pick up likely logs and sticks along the way, during the day. There are at least half a dozen *hardwoods* in Baja that burn better than store-bought charcoal: ironwood, palo colorado, mesquite, for instance. Even dried cactus is acceptable as a cooking fuel. And it burns with such a beguiling blue flame.

(Continued from preceding page)

"Upon request a Papago Indian, the guide of the party, exhibited the operation . . .

"The plant selected was about 1 meter (3-1/3 feet) high and 0.5 meter (20 inches) in diameter. Its top was first sliced off, exposing the white interior . . . It was evident that this was saturated with water, but the structure of the tissue was such that the water did not exude of its own accord. The Indian cut a stake of palo verde . . . and with this proceeded to mash the white flesh of the cactus into a pulp. As the churning progressed a bowl was formed in the top of the cactus, and when a suitable quantity of pulp had accumulated in it the Indian, taking this up handful by handful, squeezed out the water into the bowl, throwing the rejected pulp upon the ground.

"From the upper 20 centimeters (about 8 inches) of the cactus about 3 liters (3 quarts) of water was obtained. Its flavor may be described as very slightly salty and somewhat herbaceous. Any really thirsty traveler would have drunk it without hesitation, and our Papago, although he had plenty of water from the supply we carried, drank the cactus juice with evident pleasure . . .

"A bisnaga of approximately spherical form furnishes a more palatable water than the cylindrical specimens many years older, and care is taken to use for a masher a wood which has no bitter, resinous, or poisonous qualities. No deleterious effect is caused, our Indian stated, through drinking a quantity of the water, unless one subjects himself immediately afterwards to violent physical exercise . . . "

So there it is: a tip that could save your life. But please, now that you know how, don't destroy a barrel cactus just to prove it contains water — it does. Leave these life savers alone; the very one you might thoughtlessly destroy may be the one to someday save a life.

For additional information on survival, read Adolph's "Physiology Of Man In The Desert" and Edholm's "The Physiology Of Human Survival".

Tip 3. TWO FIRES: If you have a large party — especially with children — build two fires. One for cooking. One for them. That keeps kids from kicking sand on food.*

Tip 4. HOW TO START A FIRE: Don't throw gasoline on a fire to start it. Be smart: Walter takes a small evaporated milk can, cuts off the top and fills it half full of gasoline. He puts this on the ground and then puts twigs and kindling and logs *on top of it.* Wait a minute — then throw a match on it. The gasoline fumes will have permeated the wood and it catches easily. The can will burn for several minutes, so even the logs get a good start.

Another slant: for kindling, use strips torn from an old milk carton. A small pocket or trench in the ground helps keep the wind off the fire.

Or you can lay a couple of good rocks on the side of the wind so it comes through in a streaming slit that will act like a bellows. This also insures that the wind will blow smoke away from you.

Tip 5. USE A DUTCH OVEN: Be sure to bring a *dutch oven* along. I use the "Utah" type, such as the early American pioneers carried. It's a three-legged cast-iron "skillet" with a lid. The lid top has a rim around it so you can put coals on it and the food will cook on both sides. You can bake bread, stew stews, roast or fry fish or small game with it. Pies and cakes, too. So it's a skillet, stew pan, a roasting oven all in one.

An aluminum dutch oven, one-third the weight of cast-iron, is now available from Scott Mfg. Co., 3159 W. 68th, Cleveland, Ohio 44102. Lighten your load.

Tip 6. BUILD AN OVEN: When we are camped in one spot for several days I generally build an oven. (Check color photo of oven and fresh bread in chapter 9 — the oven is mostly stones and mud.) You'll need to bring only a simple grill. For the flue, knock out both ends of 4 or 5 beer cans; stack 'em up and wrap with foil. You can use foil too, for covering the piece of metal or wood used for your oven door.

*And I can't stand smokers who throw their butts around my cheffing. Food is food. Go over to the other fire . . .

Tip 7. CLEANING POTS: To keep your skillets and pans clean use salt water — and a little sand when you are camped next to the ocean. Water is scarce, remember, and often you are wise to use salt water for most of your clean-up. (Fresh water only to rinse the dishes). A salt-water soap is recommended — or one of the special dish-washing detergents, like Joy.*

Tip 8. MORE ON WATER-SAVING: Lobsters can be boiled in salt water — in fact, taste better that way. That saves your fresh water supply, too. But clams call for steaming or cooking with fresh water: you'll want to drink the broth.

Tip 9. FOILED AGAIN: Take plenty of aluminum wrap for cooking. Potatoes and corn-on-the-cob, fish, bananas, bread and many other things can be wrapped in foil and placed directly in the coals and hot ashes for baking.

By the way, we think it smart to be certain the fire is *out* before you go to sleep.

Tips for the Road

A single car or truck — traveling by itself in remote desert areas — takes a lot of chances. If a breakdown occurs — especially in hot weather — the situation could become quite dangerous.

Tip 10. CARAVAN PROTECTION: Whenever possible travel with two or more vehicles together. The one in front is always responsible for the car behind it. Watch for it in the rearview mirror. Stop if you lose sight of it. A signal should be arranged: such as the second car turning on its lights when it wants to stop the one ahead.

It's a good idea to decide on a meeting place when traveling strange country, in case you do accidentally become separated. Like: "Five miles *after* such-and-such a village." Not *in* the village, which may be crowded. After. First guy there stops at a convenient place and waits.

Tip 11. CRACK A ROCK: A large rock in the road that needs to be removed can be easily broken up by first building a fire under it - or on it.

---

*I own no stock in Procter & Gamble. I just like Joy. I used to have a girl, name of Joy. Pure Joy . . .

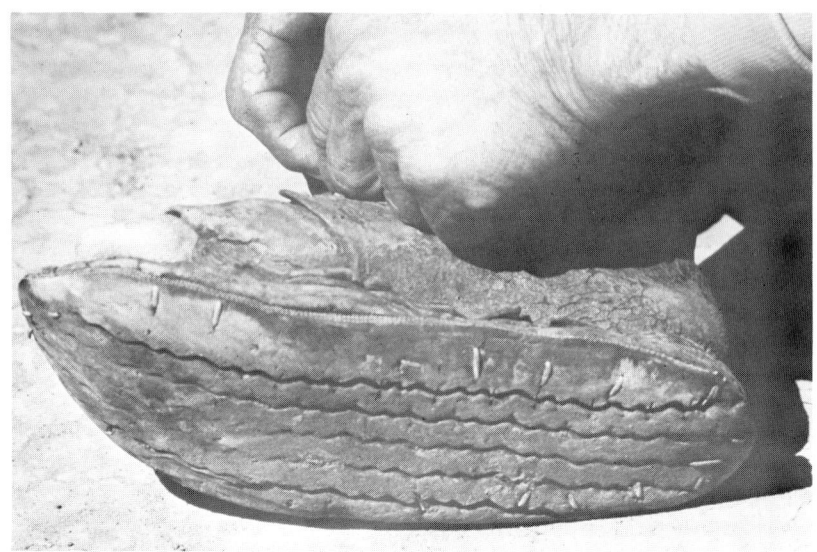

Cal Karr

Almost everything has "nine lives" in Baja; few items with any useful life are ever discarded. On the dirt tracks in Baja's "back country" you may see footprints from shoes like these; an old shoe we'd toss away is "retreaded" and provides much-needed protection from sharp rocks and cactus spines. Old tires are also cut up and used as boots and liners; they work fine where bad roads still make travel slow and tedious. Oil cans and beer cans become flower vases at remote ranchos.

Tip 12. **TIRES IN SAND**: On sandy roads, it is wise to deflate the tires down to 10 or 12 pounds pressure. It's easier on the truck — and on you. As this is an exact thing, carry a good low pressure tire gauge. Too much air won't do the job, too little may break the tire from the rim.

If stuck in the sand, a "roadbed" can be made by placing sticks and brush crosswise to the tracks, then covering these with three or four inches of sand. The sticks keep the sand from being torn out as you drive over.

Tip 13. **ON BACKING UP**: Backing on a narrow trail or in desert sand is an art every Baja driver should learn. A helper helps. The helper should take full responsibility, positioning himself where he can see the back-end of the car, the path — and, at the same time, the driver need only watch the rearview mirror to see him. If the driver is alone, better get out and walk the path carefully to memorize it. If it's a woman driver, forget the whole thing.

Tips on Impromptu Car Repairs

Mexican ingenuity adds a lot of good suggestions on what to do if your car breaks down. It won't make you as smart as that truck driver who coaxed his old vehicles over the Baja desert roads with only second gear, no generator, no water pump and no fan ... but:

Tip 14. NO JACK? If no jack is available, put a rock under the axle and dig a hole under the tire.*

Tip 15. SAVE TIN-FOIL: Head gaskets (or other gaskets) can be temporarily repaired with the tin foil from a package of cigarettes.

Tip 16. SOAP A HOLE: A small hole or crack in the gas tank or radiator can be patched for a time by rubbing a bar of laundry soap into the opening. If the gas line itself is cracked, wrap it first, tightly, with thread, then rub on the soap.

Tip 17. REPAIR A SPRING: A broken spring is temporarily repaired by jacking up the frame and wiring a four- to six-inch green log or palm frond stem in place to absorb some of the shock.

Tip 18. STARTING WITH DEAD BATTERY: Jack up rear wheel, put transmission in high, wrap rope around rear tire, turn on key, and *pull*. With automatic transmission, go fishing and forget it.

Tip 19. TO LOAD A CAR ON A TRUCK: Dig an inclined ramp next to the car. Back the truck into the hole. The car can be driven right into the truck.

Or — if the car isn't running, this is a lucky time to have a built-in hoist. A hoist is handy, too, for pulling stumps, moving other cars, pulling a boat out of the water   or maybe landing a big fish.

Fishing and Miscellaneous Ingenuity

My brother Walter had the ingenuity to wade out, stick his arm through the gills, fist forward, and land that 105-pound

---

*When you leave, fill up the hole. I may be right behind you.

totuava, back in Chapter 3. Good to remember when you have no gaff.

Tip 20. **TOO BIG A FISH?**: Heavy fish often are moved down long distances of shore line by the Mexican natives. Just tie on a good stout line and tow 'em through shallow waters.

Tip 21. **LOADING A STEER**: Again and again, you see the Mexican rancheros swim their cattle out to the boat for market, tie a line to their horns and lift them aboard on the ship's winch. (See the photo.) — A little tough on the cattle, but practical, you must admit . . .

Mike McMahan

BEEF GOES TO MARKET

Tip 22. **ROCK IN A HOLE**: When a large rock is encountered in digging a well, they simply dig a hole *behind* the rock, push the rock into *that hole* — and continue digging down . . .

Tip 23. **MAKE A REEL**: Mexican fishermen, long used to fishing with a straight line and some sort of bright lure (maybe made from an old tobacco can), had the art of swinging it around their head and making a fairly accurate cast.

Then they saw the gringo's spinning reels and saw the advantages immediately. And improvised: they took an empty plastic bleach bottle and used it to wind in their line.

Some of the natives are pretty adept with the gadget. They can play the fish by controlling the tension of the line, changing the angle according to the pull of the fish. And there are no backlashes or fouled lines and it's ready for the next cast.

You can still see these "Mexican spinning reels" all around the Gulf. They can compete with the gringo's fancy equipment any day . . .

Dad Had a Trick or Two, Himself

My Dad was a physician and surgeon up to the ripe old age of 77 and taught me a great deal about hunting and fishing back in my early days in Indiana and Texas. I guess he was proudest of the fact that he brought more than 2,500 babies into the world . . . and never lost a mother! — Back in the early part of this century *that* was an achievement.

Many a baby was delivered on the kitchen table at a farm or ranch down in Texas and once, I recall vividly, he delivered a Mexican woman while returning from another country call. She was traveling across country with her husband in an old spring wagon. Her "time" had come. Dad simply had her lie in the grass beside the road and, ten minutes later, a squealing eight-pound Mexican *niño* arrived without too many problems.

The fee? The grateful Mexican husband gave him one of a little litter of pigs from a pen in the back of the wagon.

We raised that pig with great care, I well remember. Came the first Texas "norther" of Winter, Dad decided to butcher it himself. After all, he was an accomplished surgeon — he figured he ought to know how!

That was my first lesson in anatomy — and native ingenuity. I was about nine then and the four young McMahan boys were bundled up to watch the operation under a tree in the back yard.

"About here," Dad was saying, as he dissected deeper with an expensive scalpel, "we should run into the duodenum . . . and if he had an appendix, it would be about here . . . " Most enlightening: this man was carving a future for us.

And then he showed us how to blow up the bladder and make a football out of it . . .

But, as a kid, Dad impressed me more the time — on a hunting trip near Three Rivers, Texas — when one of my young friends got a small flying insect *in his ear.*

Nothing could dislodge it and the more it buzzed around, the more the victim — Bert Archer — was going slowly out of his mind.

Dad hadn't brought his medical kit, had no instruments — and action was called for. He had Bert lie down on his side, ear up and I was instructed to urinate — as gently and as reservedly as possible — into Bert's ear.

After all, Dad pointed out this was a good saline solution and wouldn't harm the ear. It worked. Sure enough, up floated the insect and out for a breath of fresh air . . . albeit — as Bert said — slightly peeeeed off . . .

The Point Of The Cactus

Improvisation from nature is native to man, and the *bajacalifornios* have proved their ingenuity along with the rest of the world.

Baja's cactus in all its hundred-odd varieties, (80 types of Baja cactus are found nowhere else in the world) has been the source of many useful and joyful things for life beginning with that "Century" cactus plant that natives learned long ago could be turned into the potent intoxicant, *pulque.* Later generations refined it into *mescal* and *tequila.* Mescal is distilled over a wood fire and has a smoky taste like scotch. Some distillers put the maguey worm in the customer's bottle to attest to its genuine quality *"con su propio gusano"* ("with its own worm"). Tequila makes the superb drink, *Margarita,* and is very useful before breakfast at camp, to help the sun get up over the horizon.*

*One of my fishing friends also drinks it as a ritual to quiet the wind.

MEXICAN INGENUITY

Ray Haller

This sturdy native canoe is a product of mainland Mexico; it has been hollowed out of a solid mahogany log with hand labor. Mexicans have crossed the Gulf in canoes like this — but I'd rather use the modern ferry system.

From the same "Century" plant can come materials for sandals, ropes and the roof of an Indian's hut.

The "Skeleton" of the giant cardón, which grows sixty feet tall, they found could be used to make fences, corrals and even the framework for their thatched roof lean-to houses.

Baja ingenuity obviously has not been sleeping all these years . . .

Ingenuity With Language

"Health, wealth and many loves!" the Spanish toast, has a wry twist at the end "— and time to enjoy them". *Salud, pesetas y muchos amores y tiempo para gozarlos.*

So the sense of humor — sometimes outright black comedy — comes through from these descendants of Spanish blood.

The scholarly academicians may try to keep our various languages pure, but it is the twist of words that makes an idea memorable. Often in the very heat of action, the need to communicate something quickly creates richer meaning.

"Squatberry", the nickname for the laxative berry on a native bush, is only one example.

"Catarro Inglés" is their phrase for gonorrhea.*

What we call a "wetback" — a Mexican who has swum the Rio Grande for illegal entry to Texas — they call *"espalda mojada"* ("Wet shoulder"). Hitch-hikers they call *"Gente que anda con su dedo gordo"* ("people who walk with thumbs").

Baja proverbs — some borrowed from Spain, of course — bespeak the ingenuity of people with their own language. For instance, these familiar sayings and descriptive expressions:

"En boco cerrada no entran moscas" — Keep your mouth shut and the flies won't buzz in.

"Mejor ser cabrón sin que nadie lo sepa, que no lo ser cuando todos creen que eres" — "Better to be an S.O.B. and nobody knows it than not to be an S.O.B. when everybody thinks you are".

"Más sabe el diablo por viejo que por diablo" — The devil knows more because he is old and experienced than because he is bad.**

"Donde crece la escoba, nace el asno que la roe" — Where the thistle grows, there lives the ass who will eat it.

"Como telas de arañas son las leyes, que prenden a las moscas y no al milano" — Laws, like the spider's web, catch the fly and let the hawks go free.

"El amor es fuego, pero con el no se cuece el puchero" — Love is a furnace but it will not cook the stew.

"Quien teme la muerte no goza la vida" — He who fears death never enjoys life.

---

*They inherited the old Spanish custom of blaming the English for everything. In some parts of Mexico, homosexualism is called "The British Disease".

**I'm having that one carved as my epitaph.

"Triste está la casa donde la gallina canta y el gallo calla" — Sad is the house where the hen crows and the cock is silent.

"La mujer y el melón bien maduritos" — A woman and a melon, let them be fairly ripe.

How better to say it?

THE WORSHIP OF CORN

Some 30 centuries before the birth of Christ, the Indians of Mexico were cultivating maize or corn. This maize god of the Zapotec Indians (500-800 A.D.) was found in the ruins of Mount Alban, near Oaxaca, on the mainland. Note the two ears of corn. Today's Mexican menu still features corn as the staple, similar to wheat in the American diet.

TOTUAVA FROM THE PUERTECITOS AREA IN THE GULF

Walter McMahan (left) and George Mutter are happy with their fine catch; the totuava is one of the best food fishes in its family. It spawns in the upper Gulf and its normal range extends to the middle of the Sea of Cortez. The totuava reaches a length of more than three feet in three years; it is a very important species for anglers and for commercial fishermen. In recent years the annual catch has averaged around 500,000 pounds.

Campfire Gourmet:

My Favorite
Recipes

9. *Ambiance By The Campfire*
Orégano Grows Wild
How To Cook With Rocks
Cornmeal Is A Flavor
What To Do With Two Ducks
Viva La Banana: The Baja Macho

I've had better meals in the heart of Baja than at Dave Chasen's or Four Seasons or Tour d'Argent. Or so I thought, at the time.

Any camp cooking tastes great — with a pinch of ingenuity and a dash of imagination. The outdoors always sharpens your appetite — and, perhaps, the very barrenness of Baja accentuates pleasures all the more.

It is a likely place for a campfire cook's tour.

It seems to take even the tenderfoot back a few million years to our ancestors who found in the campfire protection from the strange, wild world about them — along with succulent nourishment for the inner man. Yes, the campfire thing is pretty deep in our blood.

LOBSTER FROM MAGDALENA BAY

Recipe: place grill over hardwood coals (or any coals if you're hungry) and get the coffee ready. Turn lobster as it cooks and serve with melted butter or any cocktail sauce of your choice. Dehydrated horseradish travels well in Baja, and when mixed up before mealtime, adds extra spice to bottled sauces.

Nowadays, a campfire may add something of ambiance to the dinner that a Diner's Card or Carte Blanche can't buy. The stars in those clear, clean Baja heavens are twinkling and all's right with the world. Never mind who's minding the worries back home.

I suppose my sheer enjoyment of being the campfire chef, amidst these circumstances, stems from the enjoyment I read in other's eyes, as the flames flicker up. That gleam in the eyes of Henry VIII, with a roast bird in his juice-dripping paws . . . *

I'll admit: The campfire makes a good cook great.

Orégano Grows Wild

Where else can you pick your wild orégano to season the fish you've just caught — both within a few steps of your campfire?

Let's try a little something I conjured up with the help of my friend, Ray Haller:

Fish Orégano a la Ramon

Cut   fish filets not over ¾-inch thick. Place in dutch oven.

Add   1 large sliced onion.

Chop   1 large bell pepper, and 4 fresh tomatoes, (or 1 large can).
Water, if needed, to keep filets covered throughout the cooking time.

Season with three sprigs of fresh orégano you've just picked — and salt, pepper, garlic to taste.

Time   45 minutes, approximately. Serve with toast or hard bread — and expectant glances for approval.

Catch 'Em and Cook 'Em

Never can I forget the twice-happy boyhood pride when I brought in the first mess of perch I caught in the Kankakee River. Mother showed me how to clean and fry them all by myself.

*At cooking, I'm immaculate. At eating, I'm a little slobby, like Henry.

Mother* had started us off on that toothsome Midwestern style of cooking — and she was the greatest! — but *this time* (and I don't think I saw her wink at Dad and my older brothers), she admitted my touch with the fried perch was something from which she could learn a lesson . . .

Only years later — when I was too far committed to the principle that a great hunter or a fisherman had to be equally great in preparing his "awards" for the table — did I realize her remarks could be taken two ways.

We moved to Texas. There I was to get a perspective on seasonings in food as I enjoyed ranch-style cooking and the Mexican touch on barbecue and other specialties that were robust, satisfying manna to a growing young man.

Then, in my first visits to Los Angeles, only half a life-time ago, I parlayed my bent for cooking and love of the outdoors to the job in charge of the cooking camp that, just maybe, *built* the men that built Boulder (Hoover) Dam.

Then, my first trip to Baja was heading Anderson Boarding and Supply's camp for the old "Trader Horn" movie on location in a pseudo "African locale," just South of the Border.

From then on, I was hooked. My life was certain to be addicted to fishing, to cooking and to Baja. Although, soon enough, in reverse order. Somewhere along the way, Walter convinced me I ought to earn a living, too, so that's why I joined him in the office furniture business to support my three hobbies. I figured one of us could run off to Baja while the other minded the store.

Baja, indeed, was to give a fourth perspective to my cooking. And I learned a lot from the Baja natives themselves. They have plenty of tricks.

How To Cook With Rocks

The primitive Indians of Baja ate most of their food raw. In later times, fire entered their lives, either through lightning or the

*She was the eldest of the six Alfred Brady Sibert girls of Rochester, Indiana. From her I get my German-English-Welsh heritage; Dad gave me my Irish . . . and a fifth of Scotch

special bounty of the god of Two-Boy-Scouts-Rubbed-Together. This made the larger game and fish more palatable.

And, since they had no pottery, they invented an interesting porridge; a strange assortment of wild nuts, weed seeds and acorns, which they cooked on a rock. The secret of this remarkable culinary innovation apparently came from the Indians' instinctive knowledge of heat conservation.

They knew how to *cook with rocks.*

Try it yourself: a plate-sized flat rock, heated in a quick, small fire, passes its heat back slowly for a pancake — whether made from nuts and acorns or Betty Crocker's Minneapolis-type magic.

A larger rock can cook fish or game. Just build a fire on the rock first, then sweep it off.

Soup? sure. Drop your hot rocks in the pot.*

Also, a large, flat, warm rock near your cooking fire makes a handy place to heat up plates, keep coffee and second helpings at their best.

Maybe you're the impatient lazy type who brings the prepared mixes. Okay. We've romanced Betty Crocker's Bisquick in more wild positions than the ol' gal ever dreamed of. But we still like most of these things the old-fashioned way: from *scratch*. Try Bisquick for biscuits and for pancakes, of course, and you can experiment with that "hot rock" idea and see how beautifully it works.

Cornmeal is a Flavor

You'll need cornmeal for frying fish and it can be used to extend or give variants to your biscuit and pancake recipes. Remember, simple ground corn came from Indians and Mexican Indians who knew it well 3,000 years ago. American pioneers had this — not wheat — when they traveled West. The "Johnny Cake" was of cornmeal (some contend the early spelling was "Journey Cake"). It was also called "Hoecake" (because it could be patted

*You did wash the sand off the rock, didn't you?

on the blade of a hoe and conveniently held over the fire to bake).

So don't just stand there with that hoe — cook something . . .

Cornmeal is a basic flavor characteristic to the Mexican menu today. (And most Mexicans, mainland or Baja, have a prime diet of corn and beans.) The *tortilla*, of course — that little flat, thin, pancake of cornmeal — is bread for the bulk of the population. It is the "wrapper" for tacos* to hold lettuce and meats and saucy stuffs, like a sandwich. In soft form, the tortilla wraps hot meats and gravy for a main dish. Wrap that up, it's an *enchilada*. Or you can put the tortilla in the serving plate as a base for your *huevos rancheros* (recipe later . . .) or other hot main dishes.

Crisp, by itself, the tortilla can be cracked into pieces and eaten as a snack (our American "Fritos" brand is a *variant* on this. And there are now dozens of *variants* on that particular *variant*).

Generally, you like the taste of tortillas — or you don't. You may like other breads with cornmeal, because cornmeal is so good with fish. Try this for a change:

Campfire Cornmeal Bread

Mix   1 cup cornmeal
        1 teaspoon salt
        1 teaspoon sugar

Add   1¼ cup boiling water. Stir. Heat your dutch oven or skillet. Grease with bacon fat or cooking oil.

Drop the batter, in tablespoonful sizes, into the hot grease and flatten. Cook 5 minutes. Flip, cook 5 more.

Then bring on the fish! Here's your own Hoecake or Johnnycake — and you are now a full-fledged pioneer . . .

Or leave out the sugar, put in onion flakes (or chopped onion) and sour milk, cook in deep fat — and you have good ol' Southern "Hush Puppies".

*Some say the **taco** is a gringo invention. I still say it leaks — at both ends.

Mike shows off the fresh bread baked in his quickly-constructed rock oven on the shoreline of Puerto Escondido, a favored fishing spot on the Gulf side below Loreto. Below: Pat McMahan displays some of the varieties of sea foods available to the skin diver. These were taken at Boca de Marrón, on the Pacific side near Punta Prieta.

Mike McMahan

Above: Mike and his daughter Carol ham it up beside La Burrita No. 4 at La Paz. She and her husband join Mike's explorations throughout the peninsula whenever they can.

Annual McMahan family outing to Easter Camp south of San Felipe. An afternoon surf catch of corvina.

Hush Puppies are handy because you can toss 'em across the campfire. Back in Texas, on hunting trips, the cook always threw a couple to the barking dogs. Hence the name the South dreamed up for 'em: Hush, puppies . . .

Bake Your Own Bread

Pan, bread, can be picked up at the *panaderías* in the Baja towns. They bake many good, hard-crusted European kinds. If you've progressed beyond the Bisquick stage, however, this may not fully satisfy your ego's appetite.

Back in Los Angeles, I get one of my most satisfying *enjoys* by baking my own special breads. I have a hard-working assist from my Kitchen-Aid (the only home mixer I've found that will stand up to mixing bread dough). But many times I've done it in Baja, mixing by hand.

Baja Bread

Warm large pan and put 3 cups very warm water in it.

Add 4 heaping tablespoons sugar   Mix thoroughly
2 packages dry yeast   for 3 minutes

Add 1 level tablespoon of salt and,   Mix by hand
gradually, 9 cups of flour.   for 10 minutes

Put the dough now in a warm spot with no draft for *1 hour.* (The inside of the cab of your truck, windows up, is ideal in Baja). The dough now should be risen to about twice its original size.

Punch it down for 5 minutes. Make into 2 loaves and then let it rest and place in large dutch oven (greased slightly). Cover and let rise for 45 minutes.

Bake Put dutch oven on coals, with more coals on lid to top and sides. About 35 minutes — and it's ready to serve — hot or cold.

A large-size dutch oven (size 14) is helpful when you bake bread at camp. The loaves above can be two equal "half-moons" by making a divider of flattened beer cans wrapped in foil for the center.

Or you can make your own oven from mud and rocks.

Coffee Is A Way Of Life

Mexico raises coffee, but we have an ingrown preference for the Central and South American blends. Better bring your own favorite brand — or try *Café Marino.*

And remember there are no wall plugs in the desert. Better learn to make good ranch-style coffee if you want to keep your friends.

Heat the water to a boil. *Take it off* the fire and stir in your regular-grind coffee. Cover with a lid for 5 minutes and let it steep.* (Or bring up to a good boil again, as Walter does.) Pour in about 3 tablespoons cold water, then stir again. The coffee grounds settle and it's ready to serve. No strainer needed.

Of course, you can get a dozen variations on that:

— Beat an egg white slightly and add it to the coffee grounds just before you put it in the hot water.

— You can add egg-shell to settle the grounds and mystify your friends. Some camp cooks do.

—Boil eggs in the coffee, putting them in the water from the first.

However, when you make your coffee, remember one thing: If you have Mexican guests at your campfire, they may want it served Mexican style:

Café Con Leche: Many Mexicans prefer coffee with hot milk, half and half. Heat the milk in a saucepan — but don't boil it. Make coffee separately (stronger than usual). Mix the two in the serving cup. Sugar is generally added. Sometimes cinnamon. *Café olé.*

*There's no such thing as strong coffee. Only weak people!

The Fish Dishes

There are so many ways to prepare fish, we are going to presume that as a camp cook you know most of the tricks. But, here and there a tip:

Fried Fish: We prefer bacon fat to cooking oil, as it gives fish a special flavor. That's why we always take plenty of bacon on our trips: crisp bacon for breakfast, plus a can to save the fat for the fish fry later in the day.

And, in camp, always fry your small fish with the tail on — it makes a great "handle" for eating around the campfire. A native trick is to clean fish and lay them open on the top of a metal barrel — then build a fire underneath.

Grilled Fish: With marlin or cabrillo, or any fish big enough to filet, cut your "steaks" about an inch thick. My favorite basting sauce (when time permits: also a marinating sauce) adds the extra touch of native orégano. Watch it, though, this is hot stuff.

You might want to try cooking the fish halfway, then greasing it with butter and rolling in sesame seeds. Then cook some more.

Fish On A Stick: Kids always get a kick out of grilling their own small fish on a stick. Try wrapping a piece of bacon around the fish and hooking it across the two points of a branching stick. And, in Mexico, be sure it is dry wood, not green; avoid the aromatic and toxic woods, like castor and oleander.

*Fish In Foil:** When you cook fish in foil, try a few sliced onions wrapped in with the fish. Wrap tightly in foil and cook in coals. Variation: a slice of bacon. One of my Mexican friends adds a lettuce leaf. My son Pat uses, instead of sliced onion, a good sprinkling of Lipton's dry onion soup mix. It works beautifully in place of onion in many camp recipes.

Here's one that works in Baja and equally well back home!

Walter guarantees they'll eat 'em all up. I agree . . . especially if I'm around.

*Be sure you take along an extra roll of this, too . . .

Walter's Fish Eclairs

Filet   your marlin or cabrillo or other fish, then slice each filet down to "fingersize" pieces.

Mix   1 cup flour
1 teaspoon baking powder
1 teaspoon salt
2 eggs
1 teaspoon sugar
and milk, enough to make a slightly runny mixture.

Dip   fish fingers into mixture,

Fry   in deep fat. Serve for "finger eating."

Now, let's try a fish barbecue:

Pescado Barbacoa

Cut   fish filets ½ to ¾ inch thick. Almost any kind of fish will do for this.

Marinate in 6 parts cooking oil to 1 part lemon juice — with a touch of soy and worcestershire sauce — for two hours or more.

Add   to marinating sauce:
2 onions, chopped fine
4 tomatoes, cut up in fingertip-size bits
1 can mushrooms (if available)

Season with salt, pepper, and orégano to taste. Add chopped parsley or chopped bell pepper for color. Maybe a purple Spanish onion.

Take   fish from marinating sauce and barbecue one side. Turn fish and, while second side cooks,

Strain tomatoes and parsley from marinating sauce and use to decorate the top.

    Baja natives have a trick of nailing the fish, skin side down, to a green plank or tree, then propping this against the fire.

Try The Baja Sausage — And Fish!

Chorizo is a Mexican sausage. The flavor and shape of it varies from region to region. Basically, it is the trimmings from beef and pork, with seasoning that varies. Most Baja versions are highly spiced and I really prefer milder varieties, but you can try this recipe with your own favorite sausage, regardless of type:

Fish Chorizo

Cut   fish filets not over ¾ inch thick. Place in dutch oven, greased slightly.

Top   them with a thin layer of ground-up chorizo.

Add   slices of lemon and onion rings.

Bake   on a bed of coals — with more coals heaped on top of the dutch oven, of course. About 30 minutes.

Very simple — but very yummy!

U.S. made sausage won't do for this recipe, as it generally contains too much pork fat.

What To Do With Two Ducks

Once, near Los Mochis, which is across the Gulf from La Paz, we had spent a disappointing day stalking the *pee-che willows* (the Mexican black-bellied tree duck).* We got only two. Plus two green wing teal. Hardly enough supper for our four gunsmen.

Fortunately, half the party headed out to get a little restaurant-style food at the Chapman Hotel in Los Mochis and left the ducks to Tommy and me. But fixing them was a problem. The wind was blowing like a politician's speech on the Fourth of July. And it stung with rising sand.

We decided a nearby gravel pit would be the best place to build a fire with some protection. And we knew we had to use the dutch oven or we'd have sand in the supper. But if we had to be inventive, we decided to be inventive all the way.

---

*I don't laugh at your name. Don't you laugh at his: Pichigüila.

Here's the recipe that came out of that one:

Two Drunken Ducks

First	bacon slices are set to fry up and make grease in the dutch oven.
Sauté	2 ducks rolled in flour, salt and pepper.
Add	2 bananas (the large *macho* variety preferred) 2 potatoes 1 onion 1 small can mushrooms and juice ½ cup claret wine (or ¼ cup whiskey) 5 tablespoons soy sauce, and
Sauté	until nice and brown. Put the lid back on the dutch oven. Bank with coals, top and sides and bake for 50 minutes. Tremendous.

Viva La Banana: The Baja Macho

Bananas that grow in Baja include the *macho* variety, hard — and large. The Mexicans fix them many ways and I have become quite fond of them in various recipes.

Macho means *male* and it is hardly surprising that the natives have noted the phallic design of the fruit and have given this particular type of banana certain aphrodisiac significance. *Muy macho!*

The more I use it, the more I like it.

Macho bakes well with all wild game. Fritter them as a side dish. Put them, skin and all, in the coals and ashes, then unpeel as a dessert, to be sprinkled with brown sugar.

The mango is superior as a tropical fruit, too. These are best of all *fresh* for their succulent taste. But they bake well with game, and can be baked in their skins. They are a happy component of salads, too, and desserts.

Papaya, the breakfast melon, is available in Baja. And always a pleasure.

Oranges and citrus grow in Baja — but are somewhat insipid — and are available in many markets (at the bordertowns, the chances are they came down from Alta California). But better irrigation is improving Baja's citrus yield.

Lime is more available than lemon and is to be preferred over lemon for the squeeze to sharpen the fresh papaya. Mexicans often substitute it for lemon in many of their recipes, but I've found a little bit of lime, compared to lemon, can go too long a way in cooking. Mexicans do not know lemons as we do. The lime they use for seasoning of meats and vegetables and salads, too.

Too Many Cooks Spoil The Family

Walter, I have to admit, is my only real family competition as a cook. He's a little older than I and he may have a slight edge on invention for invention's sake — but I'll battle him with dutch ovens any day.

Walter has a ranch in Escondido ("hidden valley"), on the Alta side of California — and has built there a Mexican-style hacienda with a barbecue right in the edge of the big quadrangle patio. Here a six-foot water-wheel spit can turn a couple of shoats or a young beef for the barbecue and Walter can cook for 28 Sunday guests from the Sierra Rod & Gun Club with the greatest of ease.

I have to admit he's good, but I credit Walter most of all for his inventive little touches when we're together in Baja.

Quail is my favorite game bird — much preferred over pheasant or any kind of duck — and on this particular trip, Walter, Harry and I bagged a quick dozen birds.

Walter cleaned them. Then, *through* each breast he larded a piece of bacon, weaving it in and out. Grilled — and basted with garlic butter — it was incredible.

"Quail a la McMahan" . . . try that touch of bacon any time you're lucky enough to have 12 quail for three people.

The photo above shows the small oysters which grow on the mangrove roots at Concepcion Bay, and which are revealed at low tide. They're lots of work and the edges of the shells are sharp as a razor; if you collect any wear gloves and be very careful. Below: Walter Hall, F. M. Harold and Mike enjoy a quail dinner at Puerto Escondido.

What We Learned About Baja Meats

The Mexican is only interested in how flavorful his beef is. Not how tender. We are inclined to agree and we always buy, as we cross the border, one or two of the whole tenderloins at the good meat markets in Tijuana or Mexicali.

These we do not have cut up. Meat keeps better in large pieces, we've found. Incidentally, never try to keep meat or fish in a closed air-proof plastic bag: it looks pretty — but it will spoil quickly.

The first night out, we trim the tenderloins. We cut off a few short-ribs and square the ends so they can be later cut into convenient sizes for broiling over the camp fire.

Then, for the first night, we generally have this special dish:

Carne Con Machos

Dust with flour these trimmings from the tenderloin. (Or any cut.)

Braise the meat in your dutch oven.

Add quartered potatoes and onions, and those big *macho* bananas.

Season with soy sauce, wine and orégano and other seasonings as you like. Add 2 cups water.

Cover the dutch oven with coals and let it cook while you're making camp. Ready in about 50 minutes.

An extra touch we like:

Make dumplings and add them last. The heat from the lid of the dutch oven will make them a golden brown on top, while the lower part absorbs the flavor of the stew. Zowie!

Later in the trip, you'll have your own game and fish to choose from. Here's one for the time — in the desert — when your menu comes up with one of those long, rangy desert jackrabbits. An old prospector, Jon Kune, taught me this one:

Jackrabbit Jon

Use only the upper part of the hind leg and the "saddle" or back strip of the rabbit.

Cut   the meat from the bone and pound it into small flat steaks.

Grease skillet lightly and salt it heavily.

Cook on each side for about 5 minutes.

Serve . . .

That's one you can chew on quite awhile. It's not tender — but it has a great gamey flavor you can relish with a virile red wine or plenty of cold Mexican beer.

Harry, from his international travels, specializes in things such as Japanese style steak, Poulet Roti, Veal Zurich and Huevos Rancheros. Since the last is the only one that has the remotest relation to Baja I'll include it. But only this one:

Harry's Huevos Rancheros

Cut   ham into ½ inch cubes.

Braise in skillet or dutch oven.

Add   2 cans (medium) tomato sauce. (May be Spanish style . . .)
1 tablespoon, heaping, of *Salsa Ranchera,* the Mexican *mild* pepper sauce that comes in the small, flat can or jar.
Touch of Worcestershire or soy, seasoning to taste.
As the tomato sauce starts to bubble,

Drop eggs in the sauce to poach. Cover the skillet or dutch oven so heat comes down as well as up and the steamy aroma penetrates the eggs. A spoon or two of water helps to make steam and hurry the poaching. Put a tortilla in each plate and ladle out the ham and eggs and sauce. Or use crisp tortilla bits for decoration.

Serve with beer for breakfast.

Beer For Breakfast?

Because there were no sisters* in my generation of the McMahan family, perhaps the boys all became pretty fair cooks — but each has his own tangent to the taste.

It's pretty good, I'll admit. But I think Harry invented this variation just as an excuse to have beer for breakfast. As hot as this dish is, you need the beer to cool off.

For all birds on the grill I have a little sauce trick of my own. Crushed garlic and salt, *salsa picante* (Mexican hot sauce), butter and soy sauce mixed into a fairly thick paste. Then, when the birds start to brown, I brush this on every few minutes. It gives a distinctive flavor to the game bird — and a tasty crust that is sheer poetry to the eye.

Like the Japanese, I believe that a dish should have a visual beauty all its own: appetite excitation as well as appetite satisfaction.

Salads by the Campfire

Salads? Of course. Easier than you think.

Baja — in the Mexicali region — joins California's Imperial Valley in growing the finest lettuce in the world. Then you have the superior *avocados,* for salads and for their own special place in my sun: Guacamole Salad. Let's pause a second for my favorite version — by Phyllis, Walter's wife:

Guacamole Salad

Rub   salad bowl with garlic.

Chop   avocado and onions and tomatoes into small pieces. (Do not mash.)

Season with just a taste of salt and a squeeze or two of lemon or lime. Add a dash of Worcestershire, and a pip of tabasco, perhaps.

---

*There were 3 brothers plus two half brothers. Hmmm! Now, does that add up to 4 brothers . . . or 5?

The important thing is to keep tasting as you make and season the Guacamole. Avocados, onions and lemons all vary in taste and strength. Hence precise directions cannot be given. But strive to keep the avocado dominant, with the juice of the onion and lemon to accent it.

Zucchini, summer squash and cauliflower, of course, carry well if you have picked them up along the way. Cabbage and cucumber carry better than lettuce if you are going to travel far or long.

Bell pepper keeps well and for more added color you can take the canned red pimiento. The new small, solid pack canned tomatoes (Contadina is my favorite brand) often taste better — and certainly travel better — than the fresh variety.

And that goes for the dried flake onions, too.

Let's put some of those together right now:

Tomato Salad Chapala

Pour ½ cup salad oil in a cup, with
1/8 cup vinegar and the juice from
1 large can of tomatoes.

Add 1 teaspoon salt which has been crushed and worked into
1 clove garlic (do this on a bread board with a flat knife.)

Plus 1 teaspoon sugar
— Let stand for 1 hour —

Pour over tomatoes which have been arranged in slices, with thin-sliced onions.

Garnish with parsley, chopped onion tops or tomato leaves.

A variation I do at home, sometimes, is to serve it in hollowed-out fresh tomatoes, especially when I can get the big tomatoes ripe from the farm.

Now, here's one for the Baja camp — for when you can pick up the "palms" or young tender leaves of the *nopal* cactus. These come fresh in the village markets and you can also get them canned in Baja. Maybe, if you can recognize the *nopal*, you can harvest them yourself, right by your campfire.

Frijoles y Nopalitos

Mix
1 can kidney beans, drain juice
1 can garbanzos, drain juice
1 can nopalitos (or equivalent; fresh)
1 cup vinegar
½ cup salad oil
1 tablespoon sugar

Season with soy sauce, *salsa picante,* garlic salt, according to taste. It's a meal in itself — a great salad for campfire appetites.

By the way, don't be a gullible gringo and think "salado" in Spanish means *salad* (some English words just add an "o" — but not this). *Salado* means *salty. Ensalada* is the word for *salad.*

Fool-You Lobster Cocktail

My son Pat will give his tips on skin diving and lobster catching down Baja way. But, if you don't have a lobster — and you do have certain Baja fish — you can make a sharp imitation lobster cocktail that 99 out of 100 can't tell from the real thing. Walter created the trick and here's his version:

Mock Lobster Cocktail

Filet Cabrilla, Grouper or Mero (Sea Bass). Salt it.

Wrap in foil and cook for only 4 or 5 minutes on each side so the meat is firm and flaky. Set aside to cool.

Add mustard, garlic, soy sauce, horse radish, pepper and chopped onion to taste.

Put the sauce on your "lobster" and serve.

The basic "lobster" as it comes out of the foil works almost as well in "lobster salad". But not quite.

If you're in a seaport locality and can get good fish for filets — fresh! — you may want to try it at home. Today's price of lobster keeps going up and even though Mrs. Lobster lays 50,000 eggs at a time, somehow not enough of them ever get to market. It seems other lobsters appreciate little lobsters as much as we do.

Now, quickly, a special clam recipe if you want to fancy them up just a bit.

Clam Shells Baja (Mariscos En Concha)

Cut your cooked clams into ¾-inch pieces, if large in size. Smaller sizes can be used as is.

Melt butter in frying pan; add flour and water until creamy, then grated cheese. Cook until smooth.

Stir in clam bits. Add salt and pepper.

Fill large clean clam shells with mixture, sprinkling on parsley and cracker crumbs and a thin slice of cheese and bits of butter.

Wrap the shell-and-mixture now in heavy foil (try to keep foil away from the top of the mixture) and

Bake in coals or in dutch oven. Serve individually — a half dozen each to start . . .

By now you have the idea: Lobster, small fish filets — especially the "bottom" fish like halibut — can be prepared and used instead of clams in this last recipe.

And this is my last recipe for now — at least until I make another trip . . .

The Lazy Resorts:

Travel to the Tip

10. *"The Baja Week-End" by Air*
By Car and by Ferry
Parallels: Honolulu, Acapulco, Miami
The Food is Special
How to Make a Margarita
Damiana: The Aphrodisiac
The Price is Right

There's a life of lazy luxury down at the Tip.

For the third section, the lower part of the peninsula, is almost totally different from the other two. The desert lies behind you. Now there's farming land. Lazy little haciendas, bright with hibiscus, tucked back in the hills. And lush resorts where you can enjoy a great deal of living for surprisingly little money.

The Tip — from La Paz on down to Cabo San Lucas — is due to be turned into the next great tourist center of the Western Hemisphere. Like Acapulco. It already has a great start toward its destiny.

I wish it weren't true, but it is. I've enjoyed it much too much when I had it all to myself.

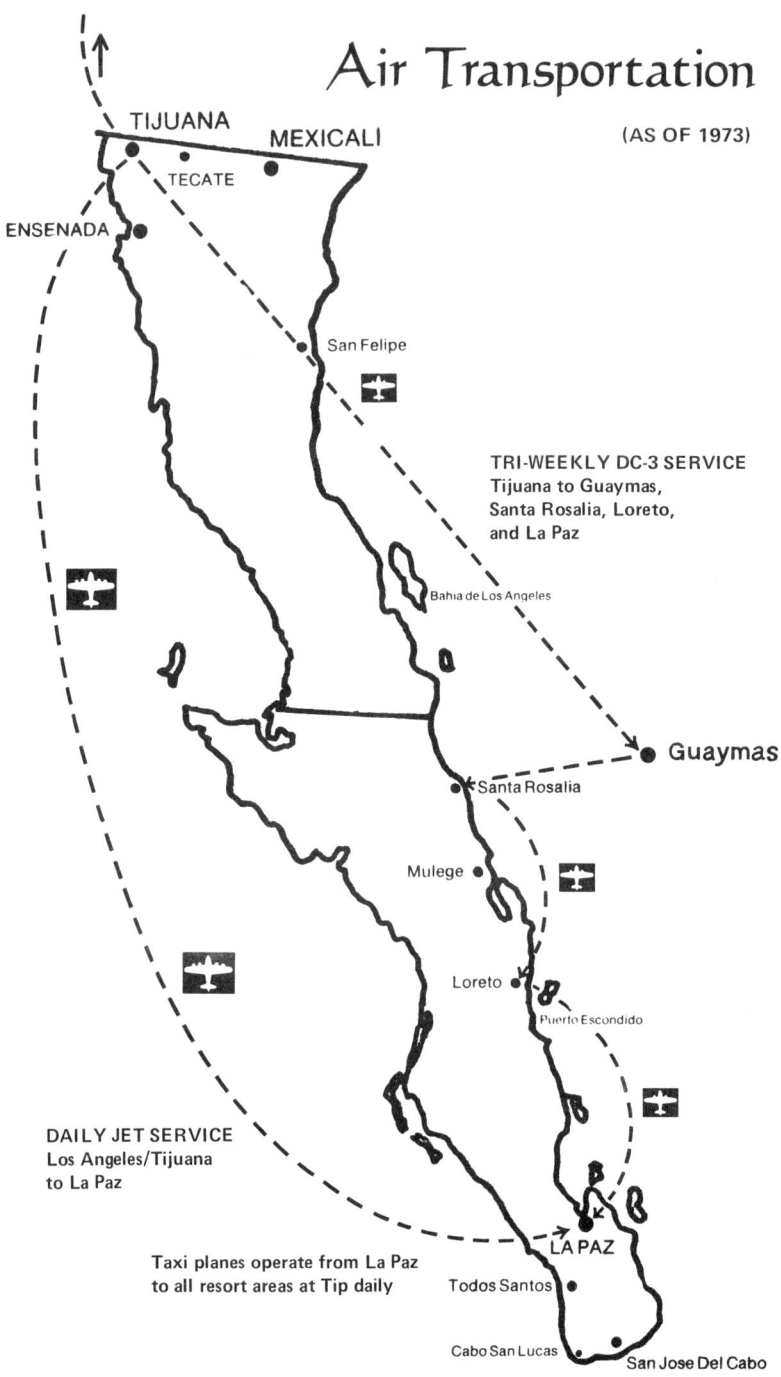

THE LAZY RESORTS

The airplane has made the "Baja Week-end" possible. The angling sportsman can fly in for a marlin on Saturday and be back at his office on Monday. If he's the kind of guy who leads that kind of split-second life.

More than 50 airstrips for private planes and the Baja air taxis dot the peninsula now — and more are constantly building. Every fisherman's lodge now has its own landing area.

And more boat harbors are being improved. In places, it's still a long way between snug harbors, but with careful planning both coastlines can now be explored by boat. Before you try this, read the books by those who've gone before you.

But now it's increasingly easy to get to the Tip by car. No, not directly down the peninsula, across the mid-section desert. Those roads are too rough for the average car.

By Car and By Ferry

Instead, you can come down the other side of the Sea of Cortéz, on the mainland of Mexico. Directly down the good highway from Nogales, Arizona.

Then, at Topolobampo or Mazatlán you take one of the auto ferries across to La Paz. And continue on your own wheels down the last 125 miles to the Tip.

It makes my heart bleed, it's so easy now.*

More roads, more ferries are in the works. And more hotels and resorts, as the Mexican government and private enterprise pour $100,000,000 or more into Baja's development in the '70s.

I can see it all now: The Hilton La Paz and the Sheraton Cabo San Lucas! Maybe you like those sky-scraper hostelries — but I bed better close to the ground. The high Hiltons give me claustrophobia and, one time in Paris, gave me dysentery.

But Progress, like a fisherman's ego, always wants something bigger. I suppose I'll have to admit there's no more likely spot on

---

*My back feels better, though. It used to take us 3 weeks by "La Burrita" over the desert.

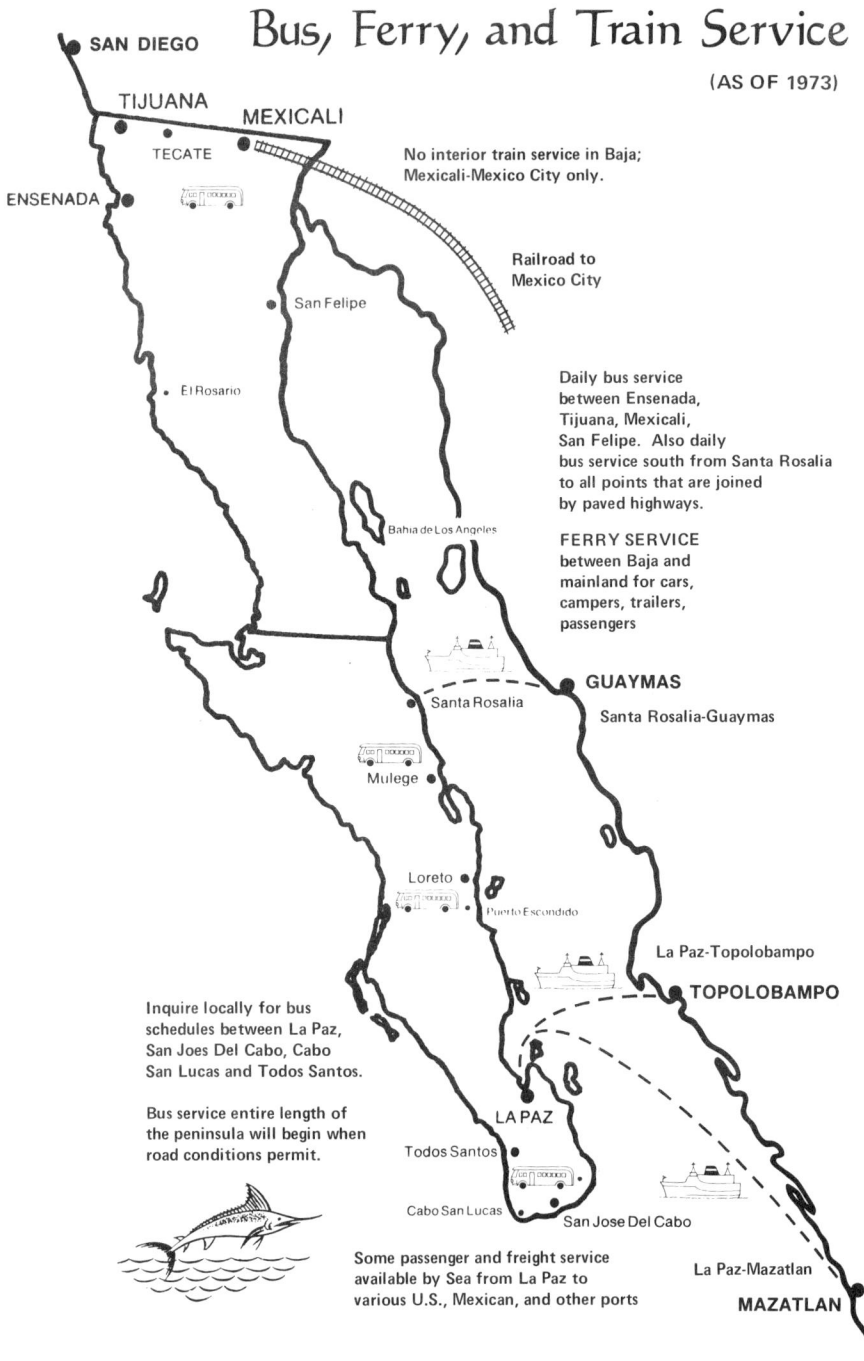

our side of the map to satisfy both. The builders and the anglers both have a perfect spot for action.

Parallels: Honolulu, Acapulco, Miami

Look at ol' Mother Earth where the map-makers have put those bands around her favorable front, where the semi-tropical breezes blow and the deep blue waters lap the sandy shores and beaches.

Between the parallels of 17° and 26° you'll find Honolulu (21°), Acapulco (17°) and Miami (26°).

La Paz and the Tip of Baja lie between 23° and 24°.

There's the big Pacific on one side and the Sea of Cortez on the other. Warm waters even in winter-time. Sandy beaches. Clear, crystal lagoons. Rocky cliffs. Low, faithful mountains. Rich, bright semi-tropical flowers.

And a lazy life of *mañana.* No telephones. No time-tables. And, *gracias a Dios,* no TV.

And fish! Let me send you back to Chapter 3 and the 800 varieties of fish that fight for a hook in the Sea of Cortez. The big ones are at the Tip — and back up the gulf all the way to Mulegé. Marlin — some more than 1,000 pounds — are in easy striking distance of the handy cruisers at the hotels. And La Paz, of course, is fisherman's haven.

If angling is not your angle, you can go off at quite a variety of other holiday tangents: Sun-drench by the pool. Stroll the long, white beaches and skinny-dip in your own secluded lagoon. And there's no one to peek at your snorkle if you want to skin-dive. Find a gem of an exotic sea-shell. Beachcomb for the Pacific treasures that find their way on down from Malarrimo.

Bird-watch if you're the peeking kind, yourself. (One naturalist, Janos Xantos, identified 92,000 species of flora and fauna at Cabo San Lucas, including 3,829 new types!). Or, if you're more the muscular type: water-ski. Ride horseback. Play tennis. Dance to a mariachi band. Do push-ups in the sand. Or why not just be lazy in the sun?

Present and Proposed Yacht Anchorages

(AS OF 1973)

As of 1973, only Ensenada and La Paz have complete services. Some of the others offer limited services and facilities; a number of the proposed anchorages do not yet offer any services.

GUARDIAN OF POOL AT HOTEL CABO SAN LUCAS

The Food is Special

Most of all: eat! The sea foods, of course, are special. And you'll find them Baja style, as well as superbly done in Continental and American cuisines at the luxury resorts and at the better restaurants in La Paz. Turtle soup. Plus steaks flown in from Kansas City and chickens from Los Angeles.*

The Baja steak has a flavor all its own, with perhaps less tenderness but much more character and taste. Even as the Argentine steak, with its pampas flavor, is wonderfully different from our grass-fed steaks, so does the Baja steer put his own brand on virility in taste. They feed on cactus and cactus builds character, I always say. We used to feed cactus to steers in South Texas by burning off the thorns with a special torch, a "pear burner". — But none of that sissy stuff for a Baja steer. He eats it,

*Some of the sports fly in their own chickens from L.A.

thorns and all. This makes awfully good steaks, but let us point out that you can't buy beef tongue — except imported — in Baja markets. A thorny problem.

Fruits? Try the tropical mango, it makes a peach blush with envy. Papaya. Bananas. Baja grapes. Figs. Pomegranates. Then have another papaya.

Drinks? The wines from southern Baja grapes are barely worth mentioning. In fact, I won't. The beers (again, you have to try Mexicali . . .) are excellent. The bars, of course, have everything from everywhere, especially the tropical drinks like planter's punch, the collinses, and so on. And the Hawaiian or Tahitian concoctions, like Dr. Funk's Big Opu or the Missionary's Downfall.*

How to Make a Margarita

But, at the end of a lazy Baja day, there's nothing quite like a Margarita. It's strictly Mexican, made with the national, native drink of tequila (distilled from the ever-useful cactus, remember?). The Margarita is an unending source of joy, a taste unique. It can make a martini go hide its olive any day.

You may want to make them later at home. So here's my recipe:

Mike's Magnificent Margarita

Chill your martini glasses in the refrigerator, of course. Then take one, rub the rim with lime (or lemon) and turn the glass upside down. Dip in salt (sprinkled out on a napkin, say). The moist glass will pick up just enough salt to *rim* the glass. Ah!

Mix 4 parts tequila,
1 part cointreau, Triple Sec — or *Damiana*
1 part lime (or lemon) juice.

Stir over ice.

Pour gently into that prepared glass, and it's a wonderful world . . .

---

*Or Acapulco's exotic **Coco Loco** or Crazy Coconut. Just make a hole in the coconut and pour in tequila . . .

CLIFF–SIDE RESORT CATCHES SUNSET VIEW

At the Tip of the Peninsula many new resorts are opening. This, the Finisterra, cliff-side to catch the sunset where the Pacific comes in to meet the Gulf. Most resorts have their own boats for marlin fishing. Some also have airports.

By the way, you know why we clink glasses when we drink another's health? The Baja sophisticate can tell you:

The wines and other charming intoxicants of the world should appeal to all our senses as they brighten our lives. We can taste them, touch them, smell them, see them. But we can't *hear* them ...

Clink! I drink your health!

"Salud, pesetas y muchos amores y ... tiempo para gozarlos!
"Health, wealth and many loves ... and time to enjoy them ... "

Damiana: The Aphrodisiac

You'll want to try Kahlua, Mexico's coffee liqueur, and the hotel's bar may have that superb drink from Peru — *Pisca* — for a Pisca Sour. But there's one other drink that is Baja's own, for only in the lonely stretches of this peninsula grows the plant that makes it: Damiana.

Damiana is a fetching little bush with yellow flowers. It looks like orégano and it grows wild at the southern end of the peninsula. Since primitive times, the natives have believed it has aphrodisiac qualities. They drink it as a tea.

Of course they had learned to ferment and distill the juice from cactus for pulque, mescal and tequila, so it didn't take long to do the same with damiana.

At the turn of the century, Winder & Shearer made "Damiana Bitters" in San Francisco and labeled it "The New, Wonderful & Only Certain Aphrodisiac".

Today, you cannot buy Damiana in the States, perhaps because of that reputation as an aphrodisiac, perhaps because it now says, "Want That Volcano Feeling?" In Baja, yes. Get your bartender to use Damiana instead of cointreau in your *Margarita*.

That is, if you're not alone . . .

The Price is Right

Are the luxury places expensive?

No. Even with all the fine food included, the prices run far less than the equivalents in New York or Miami. But call your travel agent or your broker for currently inflating quotes.

Each resort has its own individual charm in the world of leisure. The older, better ones are in Spanish tradition and may offer rambling verandas and porticos with bouganvillea blossoms trailing over with a splash of color. Stone-covered walls. High, vaulted rooms. Often there are onyx baths — with the marble from the old Baja mines at El Mármol or El Marmolita. Private guest houses. Private beaches. Swimming pools. And service you haven't seen lately even in the European spas.

Hotel Palmilla, the oldest — and some think the best — is near the tip. The Finisterra is one of the newest and most luxurious. Hacienda Cabo San Lucas is on land's end. Hotel Cabo San Lucas is between the two. The similarity of these names sometimes confuses their guests; the second may sometimes add: *Camino Real*.

Above: The lower part of the peninsula, as it appears from 125 miles out in space. This photo was taken by the astronauts; reproduction here through the courtesy of NASA and the Technology Application Center.

Right: First day's catch by Diana McMahan at Punta Colorada near the tip. Shown here are her Marlin and Dolphin fish; she also caught a Roosterfish that didn't fit into the picture. All are spectacular gamefish to catch, and the Dolphin fish is a gourmet's delight at the table.

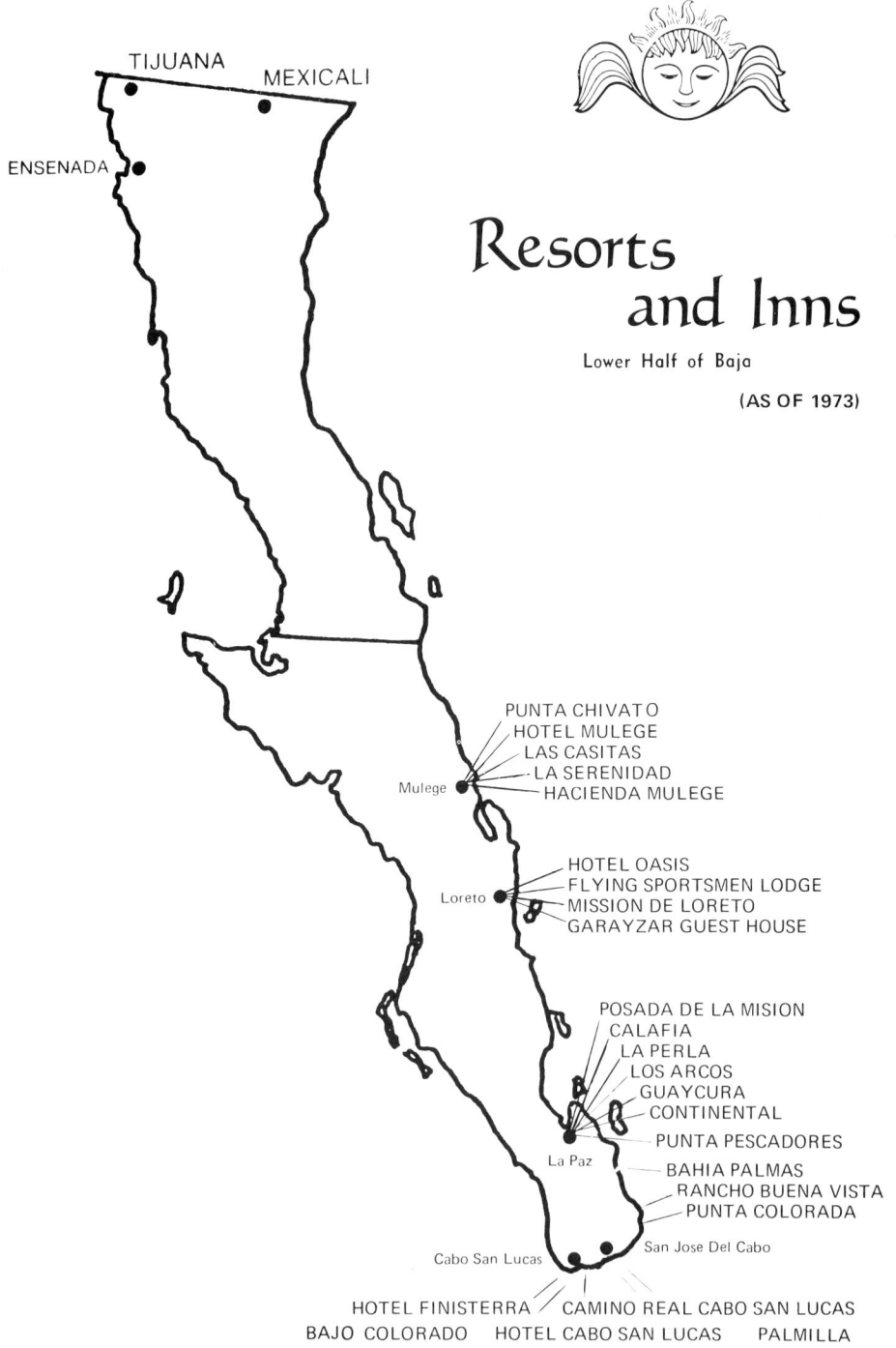

THE LAZY RESORTS

Others, large and small, are building all over the cape.

At La Paz, the new *Hotel Continental* is being completed as this ink dries. Nothing else there quite approaches the "luxury" class, but there's good comfort, food and fisherman's luck at such older, established hostelries as La Posada, Los Arcos, La Perla, the Guaycura and the Calafia.

In between La Paz and the Tip, about 90 miles down on this 125 mile distance, is a rather new hotel — but still in comfortable old Baja style. It is one of my favorite spots, Hotel Punta Colorada, a friendly inn high on the bluff, run by Bob and Cha-Cha Von Wormer. Just south of there* is just about the best of five choice surf fishing spots in all Baja.

Along the way from La Paz to Hotel Punta Colorada you'll find at least three very comfortable spots: Punta Pescadores, Bahía Palmas and Rancho Buena Vista. Tab that last one for live bait fishing. Prices there will run about half the cost of the top resorts but they'll make you very happy if you're there mainly to enjoy the superb fishing in these waters.

And they'll cook your catch or arrange to deep-freeze or smoke your fish, if that's your pleasure.

Some Other Places to Stay

New ones are springing up like rabbits as soon as you've run out of shells. Again, as I say, see your travel agent for the latest line and quotes. Except for the three/four "luxury" spots you find the prices drop as much as when you go from a better New York hotel to spend the night in Memphis.

North of the Tip in Baja it's fairly difficult to find anything else that approaches "luxury" in classification. Fine accommodations, yes. Perhaps a few that you may become especially attached to because of the host's hospitality or the creature comfort or the style of cooking. Near Loreto, we've become so attached to the Hotel Oasis because of Bill and Gloria Benzinger. Puerto Escondido — one of the most beautiful spots in Baja, has plans for a resort. Many flying fishermen like the Flying Sportsman Lodge, in Loreto, where you might try a cast from your seaside bungalow.

*I'm not going to tell you the exact mileage. I'd just as soon you get lost . . .

Aeronaves de Mexico

Beautiful swimming beaches, marlin fishing and surf fishing, there's something for every taste along the shoreline near the tip. This is Rancho Buena Vista, where the day's catch of marlin has just been weighed and the happy anglers are ready to relax. Marlin are plentiful in the tip region.

Hotel Punta Chivato, above Mulegé *(Moo-lay-hay)* is a newer hotel with air-conditioned rooms, its own fishing fleet and skin-divers shop. There are at least four or five other good accommodations in Mulegé for the flying fishermen.

Turtle steaks are a specialty with Antero Diaz at Los Angeles Bay. Prices are moderate; a pleasant but not luxurious resort which is popular with those who can fly in. As the roads are improved, more and more campers are certain to sample those wonderful turtle steaks.

It depends a great deal on what you want to do and what you want to spend. Rest assured, much of that $100,000,000 investment in guest accommodations and facilities in Baja will find a way to please you.

But it will be difficult for some of the newer ones to approach the special feeling that the innkeeper himself has given to the old.

And among all the "innkeepers" of Baja there must be two women especially enshrined in our memories, Hattie Hamilton and Alberta Meling.

The Hamilton Ranch — and Hattie

Today the Hamilton Ranch is a guest ranch not too far from the old Mission Santo Domingo, about 80 miles down and in from Ensenada. Hunters use it as a base for hunting expeditions into the Sierra San Miguel to the east and the higher Sierra de San Pedro Mártir.

But, originally it was one of the early American ranches founded — by Randolph Young — back before the turn of the century. It survived the Revolution in 1911 and eventually came into the hands of the remarkable Harriet "Hattie" Hamilton. She could shoot with the best of hunters — and outcook us all. She was in the Old West tradition, every inch a pioneer woman. Today's woman's liberation movement could have used her, too.

But Hattie has gone on to her reward in that Great Big Game Hunt in the Sky. Someday, somewhere up there, I hope she meets up with Annie Oakley and Calamity Jane. It would be the match of two centuries. For Hattie was one helluva good shot. And she knew how to cook what she shot.

The Meling Ranch's "Miss Bertie"

And Alberta Meling was cut of the same cloth. Solid fabric, a texture of leather, a touch of satin. As a girl from Texas, she had come to Baja with her father in 1897 to develop a placer mine. Fourteen years later, revolutionists forced them to flee to San Diego; the outlaws burned nearby ranches, killed cattle and stopped the mines. (But Alberta's two brothers stayed behind to fight, chased the bandits and wiped them out in a bloody gun battle.)

In San Diego, Alberta met Salvador Meling — a Norwegian émigré who had been trying his luck in Baja too. They were

Dolly Maw

"MISS BERTIE" — REVERED AND REMEMBERED BY ALL RANCH GUESTS

married and, together, in 1919 they started the Meling Ranch*, not too far from the Hamilton spread, more into the mountain country itself.

"Miss Bertie's" face, a half-century of Baja later, I'd call a fit subject for a sculptor — bronzed with the wind and sun of a land she conquered in pioneer fashion. Whether Baja ever adopted her, she adopted it. She, too, was the dominant figure in their guest ranch, overseeing the sheep and the cattle and the pigs with a cook's eye view. The abundant game in the hills, the ducks in the sky, the trout in the mountain stream — all had equal intrigue for ulterior purposes on her belt-busting dinner tables.

She was equally at home with a scientific expedition based at her ranch, a newlywed couple on their Baja honeymoon or a pair of gullible gringos with another "lost treasure" map of the mountains beyond.

*Their son, Andy Meling, in 1963 started out with 9 venturesome friends and 20 reluctant mules to prove they could travel the length of the peninsula that way. The trek took them 1,500 miles and many months, and only Andy and 1 guest, Joanne Alford, completed it. Thirteen of the mules had to be replaced, 1 died of weed poisoning. And 1 was killed by a mountain lion. Moral: fly!

A master story-teller, she had lived and played her part in the exciting pioneer times she described so well. Inn-keeper? There couldn't be a better one.

That, at least, is something I have that you can't have: the rich, vivid memories of Hattie Hamilton and Alberta Meling. Two great pioneer women the like of which you youngsters may never know.

"Mi Casa es Su Casa"

So . . . a Baja Baedecker this isn't . . .

Some want that luxury resort. Some want only a tourist court to catch a few hours shut-eye before the fishing boat pulls anchor at dawn. Me, I'm apt to prefer a sleeping bag and the stars above, anywhere along the way. Baja offers sleepy-heads an infinite choice.

"Mi casa es su casa" — My house is your house.

And where else, I *ask* you, can you find — so near and yet seemingly so far — a foreign land so strange, where every new dawn can bring so many surprises?

You don't *have* to learn the language — but you'll have even more fun if you try. You don't *have* to change your money, but pesos are more practical if you stray far from the pavement.

All you really are certain to change is your point of view: you'll come back with a deeper understanding of a most fascinating people and their challenging way of life, where every friend you make will want to share with you the best of everything he has. At first, you'll find Baja's people polite but very reserved. But once you reach their hearts, there are no finer friends. Then it's really true — *"Mi casa es su casa"*.

BAJA "GROWS" GOOD FISHERMEN

Mike's son, Pat, and his friend, Mike Pitcher, have been going to Baja since they were about five: fishing, hunting, surfing, skin-diving. Between the two pictures of Pat & Mike there is 15 years. That's Marty Johnson (on left) who's joined them in lower photo.

Mike McMahan

Skin Diving:

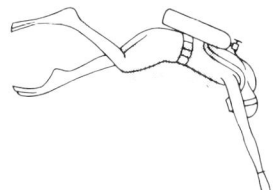

My Son, Pat,
the Expert

II. *Lobsters, East and West*
Pat on Native Techniques
How to Find Where the Action Is
Spearing the Sportfish
Halibut, Abalone, Scallops, Clams
Who's Afraid of Sharks?
Jellyfish and Other Nuisances

What's the difference between East Coast and West Coast American lobster?

The tasty, delectable pincer claws. Maine lobsters have 'em. California's don't.

What's the difference between Baja's Pacific Spiny and the *Caribe* or *Cortez* (pinta) lobsters?

The tasty, delectable tail. The two-pound Pacific has a one-pound tail. The two-pound Cortez has a half-pound tail.

— For such succulent information, I have to turn to my son, Pat, the skin-diving expert.

Since Pat was five years old, he's been making the Baja runs with me and, now that he's past voting age, he's better than a green hand at just about anything Baja has to offer. Hunting. Fishing. Exploring. Skin Diving. Spear Fishing.

Camp Cookery, too. I helped a little there. But Pat is the kind of Young Turk who has to compete always, and try to top Ol' Dad.*

The underwater bit with snorkel or aqua-lung and spear happens to be his thing. He even wrote a college thesis on the subject of lobsters and how to catch 'em. It's worth a briefing here and now:

PAT COMPARES GULF (LEFT) AND PACIFIC LOBSTERS

Gulf lobster on the left is about the same length as the Pacific, but its tail is smaller and contains less meat.

How to Tell One Lobster From Another

Pat's dissertation on the subject has these points and tips to make, so let's pass them on to you in his own informative language:

*Lately he's been taking Cordon Bleu cooking lessons. I think he plans to out-cook me in three languages yet.

The Pacific Spiny is distributed all down the West (or Pacific) shore line, almost to the Tip. But not in the Gulf of Cortez.

The Cortez lobster overlaps a little on the Pacific side. From Magdalena Bay (about 150 miles north of the tip) its range extends down the Pacific side and around the Tip, then on up the Gulf side as far as Los Angeles Bay, providing good sport along another 400 miles of interior shoreline.

Warm currents keep the Pacific Spiny out of the Gulf. Cold currents slow the Cortez lobster from going on up the West side beyond Magdalena.

For commercial purposes, the Pacific variety is preferred to the smaller Cortez or *pinta* lobster, so commercial boats rarely go below Magdalena Bay. There the catch is about 75% Pacific, 25% Cortez. Local boats take the smaller lobsters for local use.

The Pacific lobster is red. The Cortez is dark, bluish black. Both are good eating. Neither is as tasty, a New Englander* would say, as the Maine lobster. The Maine lobster has those claws, grows to a larger size, has more meat.

A plan is now in experimentation in San Diego to stock Eastern lobsters in Pacific waters. It is impossible to interbreed the two species, however, as the spiny lobster has external fertilization, the Eastern has internal fertilization. It seems East is East and West is West and never the twain shall meet . . .

Pat on Native Techniques

Baja's native fishermen generally take their catch at night, with a long spear, in from two to five feet of water.

A strong light is needed. Natives first developed this trick, using a torch-like receptacle in which they kept little twigs and grasses burning. Kerosene lamps, gasoline lanters and today's high-powered electric torches have progressively made this task easier.

---

*Brother Harry, who now lives in Rhode Island, says it. We Westerners don't.

The lobsters are "night people" and, like most other free-swimming sea life, will not frighten as easily at night as they will in daylight — even in the strongest artificial light. Too, they have lousy eye-sight and depend on their antennae "feelers" to give them their direction.

The Cortez lobster spends his daylight hours in the shelters of caves or crevices. At night he wanders in the shallow waters where the waves churn up a gourmet's choice of algae, protozoa and organic tid-bits.

The native places his spear in the water before he aims it, thus noting the refraction of the image in the water and so increasing his accuracy.

In the daytime, lobsters also can be taken by hand. But wear gloves. Cotton, pigskin, or the heavy canvas gloves used by beekeepers are best for protection against the sharp and sometimes poisonous spines* and barnacles on the lobsters and surrounding rocks.

How to Find Where the Action Is

The clear waters of the Gulf make it easy to find a likely lobster cave. Look for a bare, rocky bottom, with no thick seaweed at the lobster's doorstep. It should be exposed to the ocean currents.

If there are fish swimming in and out of the cave, forget it.

Generally, lobsters prefer a home position that faces the current, often on the downhill side of the sea bottom so the water will bring the food to them.

The lobster cave may be only two feet under the surface at low tide, but 5 to 25 feet is a more likely range. However, Cortez lobster are occasionally taken at 45 feet and have been reported at 75 feet.

---

*Pat ran a hunk of poisonous coral — very rare — into his thumb while lobster-diving near Loreto. It cost him a week of his vacation, seven doctors' bills and 20% of his thumb before the throb quieted down from a roar. Now he wears pigskin gloves.

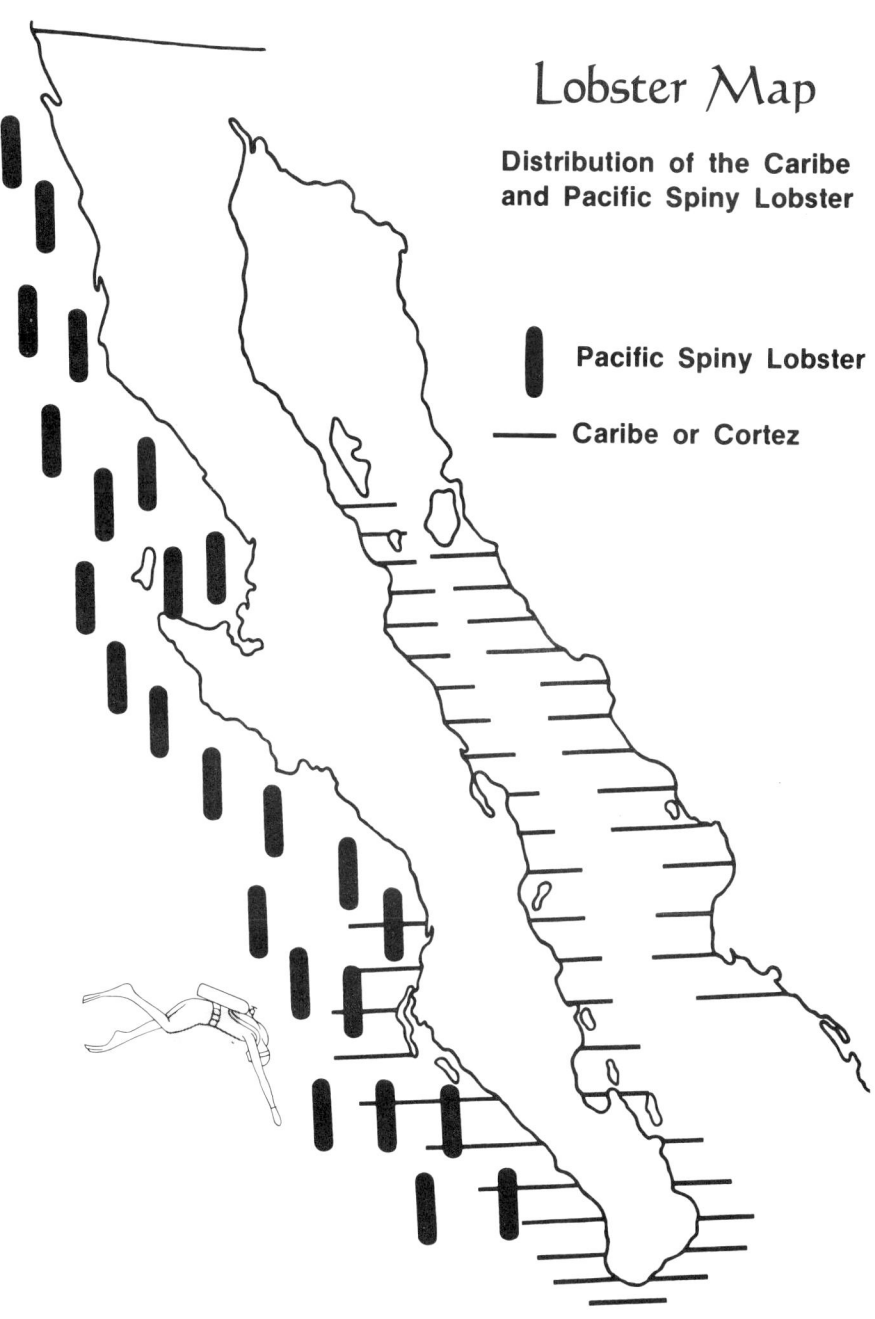

Before diving, plot your route. You may bring up two – even three lobsters – on a single dive. Pat brought up 4 in a single dive in 1970.

Look into each likely crevice. If a lobster is there, try to check-see if he has an escape route. That is the way he is apt to head.

But grab him before he starts to move. Once in motion, he is faster than you can ever be.

If you see only the lobster's feelers, start by waving your fingers near their tips. Don't touch yet. He'll get curious and investigate. Then, as he comes out, grab him.

Two-man method: One dives, one watches from above. Diver pokes a stick in possible homes. Man above observes and spots the lobster as he runs out. He'll go about 15 to 25 feet — then stop and "freeze". (He'll hold still for two or three minutes, expecting his coloration to save him.) The man above then signals location to the man below. Pick 'em up . . .

Pacific and Gulf lobsters (unlike the Eastern types) are, by and large, gregarious and often travel in groups. Some holes he's seen, Pat reports, have as many as 25 lobsters.

Sex Life of the Lobster

Pat thinks it is important for us to know something of the sex life of the lobster. So, let's be Peeping Toms and I'll add my own observations:

The female lobster gets in the mood maybe once every two years. She will lay some 50,000 eggs in her little egg-basket for the coming of the male.

He makes one deposit. Pay day! She handles it like a bank, keeping it handy in that little receptacle while laying more of those 50,000 eggs. A fringe of hair has a sort of "egg-glue" to keep the eggs tethered to her body.

And then she'll carry the eggs — sometimes, 4 months or more while the deposit earns interest. Before the time the lobster babies are the size of very small peas — curled up, doubled up, with their two little eyes facing out — she lets them loose on their own.

Chances for survival, of course, aren't even one-in-a-thousand.* But that's life.

The biggest enemies of these little lobsters are big lobsters. And a big lobster will, especially during the shedding season, fight with any other lobster that crosses his path.

Winner take all: lobster dinner! For to the lobster, as to man, the greatest seafood delicacy of all may well be another lobster . . .

Spearing the Sportfish

Spearfishing is a sport all its own. And Southern Baja has just about the widest choice: rooster fish, toro, cabrilla, tuna, skipjack, amberjack and others.

There are several principles that Pat finds successful in spearing the sportfish.

Spotting: Find a rocky area near shore about 15 to 40 feet deep where small fish congregate. Early morning and late afternoon are best. Midday, so-so.

Scout around until you find a large school of bait fish. Larger fish will mingle in with the smaller ones. Or swim along until you spot a large rock or cave. Often big fish sleep in crevices or at the side of the rocks.

Kick with a continuous, even stroke. Do not splash loudly. Once a large fish is spotted, stop kicking and descend below the surface, allowing your momentum to carry you down the first few feet.

Head toward the fish, gun ready, kicking evenly. If you cannot get within range, 3 to 5 feet, come to a stop and lie suspended. You might try hitting your shaft against the gun as noise often attracts the fish and he may turn and swim closer to you.

*It's closer to 1-in-9,000.

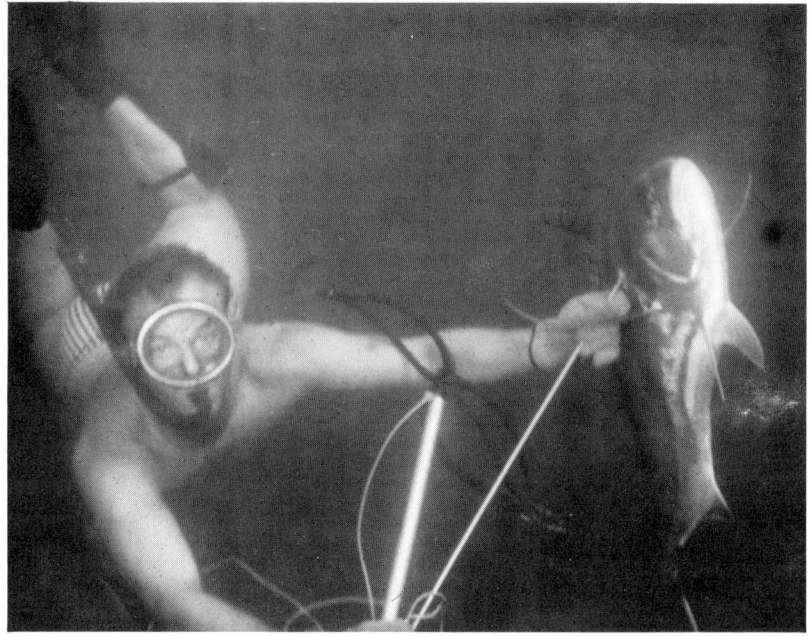

Aim for a vital area. If he is facing you: between the eyes or back an inch or so. Sideways: above the pectoral or side fin.

When you hit either of these spots the fish likely will be stunned and the meat saved. Return to the surface for air and pull yourself down the line to grab the fish. (On sportfishing, it is best to use less than 20 feet of line, so they can't swim too far away or hide in a cave.) Land him as soon as possible. Often a stunned fish regains consciousness a minute or two after hit.

Spearing the Big Ones

Black sea bass, grouper, totuava, jewfish and the other big ones require heavier gear, more speed, more shooting accuracy.*

The hunt is longer when the fish are fewer. But the reward is greater. When breakaway gear is used, the line from the shaft is attached to a flotation device on the surface. The fish then fights the float.

On the other hand, the line mounted to the gun gives the spearsman more fun in playing and he can keep the fish from running for that cave.

*And a helluva lot more work, says Pat.

This is a good-sized grouper, one of the best-tasting fish divers can obtain. Pat's fun provides dinner for the whole gang.

Sea turtles are a special game. In Baja, the *Caguama* run from 20 to 250 pounds. The *Carey* is a smaller variety, more valued for its shell — although it makes a fine soup, too. (And turtle steaks, breaded and fried, are a pleasant memory of the battle!)

Best way to get a turtle: Speed is important, as they remain still only a short time and are much faster than you expect. You must get close — in a 3-to-5 foot range — to penetrate the shell at a right angle with a double-band gun. Hit directly between the crown of the shell, and the edge near the head.

Once speared, grab him by the head and tail sections of the shell and steer upward. The rear legs will keep kicking and propel you to the top.

Keep clear of his mouth. He bites.

Halibut, Abalone, Scallops, Clams

Pat's spear techniques work for halibut, pargo and other "bottom" fish, as well. When the water is clear, it's easy.

Frank Small digging hacha clams at low tide, Puerto Escondido a few years ago. Now you have to dive for them.

Abalone can be had for the picking. Or prying. (On the Pacific side only. The waters of the Gulf are too warm for 'em.)

Clams and scallops are available on many of the beaches: just a simple dig. Rock oysters are available in some lagoons.

Near Loreto, on the Gulf side, you may find the *Hacha* clam, a giant hatchet-like clam that has a shell more than a foot long.

Our favorite clamming place is at San Quintín, down the Pacific side of Baja, about 130 miles south of Ensenada. The McMahan clan has an annual clambake down this way each Easter or so. With butter clams and the larger delicious Pismo clams.

The beaches at San Quintín and along the coast nearby are excellent. The protected waters of the bay offer boating and fishing fun even when strong winds make the open sea dangerous for small boats. And in season, the bay is popular with hunters who come there for brant and ducks.

The swimming and surf-fishing are especially good in this bay. Kids love the clamming; squishing the sand between their toes, "feeling" them out, and coming up with a nice fat clam in their hands. Grown-ups too.

Clamming is good on the Gulf side of the peninsula, at the Bay of Los Angeles, Concepción Bay, the Bay of La Paz and at the Tip, along with many intermittent spots in between.

All you need is a spading fork and a bucket. Invert the fork and drag it across the surface of the wet sand. Every time you hear a "click" you've struck a clam. You should fill your bucket in a short time.

Get the sand out. Easiest way to wash is with two buckets, changing water often and agitating thoroughly until the last bucket of water shows no trace of sand. Throw out the empty half shells as you wash.

Then, it's a good idea to let the clams set in a bucket of salt water for a few hours. They'll continue to "rinse" themselves, jetting the water and sand out of their shells like a Texas cowpoke with a cud of chewing tobacco.

Then put the clean clams in fresh water, add butter and a little parsley. (Or you may prefer mace, thyme or orégano.) Bring to a boil for 3 minutes and they're ready to serve, in the shell.

Serve a heaping plateful for each clam-eater. He opens one, digs out the clam inside and dips it into the broth (served in individual cups), dips again in melted butter and WHAP! — down the hatch!

If you have any left over — we doubt it — save them for breakfast and try chopped clams in scrambled eggs or omelet.

Who's Afraid of Sharks?

The shark has gotten a reputation he doesn't entirely deserve. Many writers have over-dramatized the presence of sharks in shallow water. The man-eating shark is a deep water fish rarely found in depths of less than 50 feet.

So the diver who is working in the shallows offshore from Baja has practically nothing to fear. But just in case — in that unusual instance they never mention in the travel folders — you run into Mr. Shark, here are a few points to remember:

Don't panic. Fear is your first danger.

The shark uses three senses in finding his food.

1) Smell. He can smell blood hundreds of feet away. So, try not to bleed.

2) Sound. He can hear a crippled fish splashing far away, on the surface. So, cut down your kicking strokes on the surface.

3) Sight. Here he's weakest, as tests show a shark can see only up to ten feet. This is why the shark is really a slow, lackadaisical creature, approaching with caution.* He circles and sizes up his dinner-to-be. So, while he's doing that, *think: don't panic, don't splash. Submerge, swimming at him as fast as you can and scream!* Yes, strange noise has been known to frighten sharks away.

Story: a pilot, shot down at sea in World War II, was attacked by a shark three times. Each time he jumped on the shark's head and pushed him down in the water as the shark swam by. The shark, finally discouraged and baffled, went away.

Maybe. Try it. Let us know if it really works . . .

Jellyfish and Other Nuisances

The octopus looks much uglier than he acts. In Baja waters he is often no larger than your fist. He dines on baby lobsters, crabs and fish. No problem to you. In fact, you can become rather fond of the little beggars. But it is not wise to let them become attached to you . . .

Sea-lions, too, are much more ferocious-looking in appearance than performance. In fact, they need the full protection of all ecologists, as certain interests have been slaughtering those that live on these Pacific shores. They are

*Go thou and do likewise.

SKIN DIVING

commercially useful to the Chinese, who import vital organs of the sea lion from Baja to use in making their own high-demand virility drugs.

A minor irritation is one of the common varieties of jellyfish, a cousin of the Portuguese Man-of-War, in Baja waters. It can be found, unfortunately, most often between Loreto and Cabo San Lucas. At times, a dangerous nuisance.

There he is — and very hard to see — a blue bubble barely more than a half-inch in diameter, with a cobweb of poisonous strings underwater. These may be ten feet long, with a toxic little water-drop poison bead every foot or so.

If he slaps you with one of these strings you may have welts on you for the next eight hours — and your stomach will be a fireball of pain.

Aqua Malo, the natives call him. And they have a herb or two that helps to kill the pain. Or use a little common ammonia.*

Moray eels are ugly-looking little monsters that are potentially dangerous. The snake-like Morays are often found in the Gulf and at the Tip, swimming among the rocks. In the colder water of the Pacific, they are seldom seen in daytime away from their protective caves.

The Morays love lobster, and have been known to share lobster caves. Rare, but watch it. And wear those pigskin gloves.

Stingrays are occasionally found in the shallow surf of sandy beaches. They have a nasty habit of whipping up their dagger-like tails to sting you around the ankles. Mildly poisonous and quite painful. Soak your feet in hot water and epsom salts.

And soak your head for not being careful.

There's so much to enjoy on the 2,861 miles of sea shore around Baja that it's a shame to let these little nuisances spoil your fun.

---

*If neither is available, Pat recommends a little urine on your handkerchief. Apply to welts. You should feel relieved now . . .

If you're a skin-diver, surf fisherman, shell collector or just a beardy beachcomber, Pat and I bid you welcome to the club.

And the real treasure of the Baja bays and beaches may simply be just in being there. Thinking about how nice it would be to do something and being lazy about doing it. Clamming at San Quintín. Finding that sea shell. Bringing up four lobsters in a single dive. Wrestling a turtle. Pulling in fifty pounds of sportfish through the surf. Or taking a naked dip in a blue lagoon.

But, most of all: just being there . . .

Ray Haller

CLEANING PISMO CLAMS AT SANTA MARIA BEACH

They're large, and delicious, and available along many of the fine sand beaches in the San Quintín area. These were dug along the gently-sloping beach near Santa Maria, just below Bahía de San Quintín. North of this area, San Antonio del Mar is another popular spot for Pismos. If you have a dune-buggy or any off-road vehicle which can handle the sandy beaches in this area, it's possible to drive along the beaches when the tide is going out and dig for clams at low tide in the more remote areas. But don't stay too long; make sure you get back to a point where you can leave the beach before the tide comes in.

The Peripatetic Padres:

Fiestas,
Frustrations,
Footnotes

12. *Fiestas & Festivals*
25 Steps to Alta California
The Ruins of Santa María
Jesuits Out, Franciscans In
The Indians Kill a Priest
The Father Who Fathered a Village
Pot of Gold in a Mission Wall

You have to thank the good priests for giving Mexico its great fiestas and festivals.

Sure, many Mexicans blame the Catholic church for having owned half the land and buildings at one time and for having taken advantage of the poor Indians in forcing them to give the time and the labor it took to build the ornate churches.

But credit the padres with basic dedication and determination. They weren't a bunch of simpering religious fanatics. Not in Baja. These were men of guts. They had to be, to survive in this barren, desolate peninsula.

Methinks you have to give the padres more credit for courage than you do the conquistadores and the early explorers. But history writes it the other way — as history so often does — in praise of warriors.

THERE IT IS: BAJA!

The padres set out to build a chain of missions up the Baja peninsula and, later, step by step, through Upper California.

Each was to be a day's journey to the next.

Each was to be church, farm* and cemetery — and sometimes, hospital, arsenal, barracks, school and meeting place for a native population that probably couldn't have cared less.

Spain sent out conquistadores and padres in tandem. The Sword and the Cross. Queen Isabella had wrangled from the Pope the right to select the men for all Church offices. So all priests were financed by Spain until they could live off the land. With the soldiers, they conquered Mexico. They conquered Perú.

But Baja was to turn the tables.

Fiestas and Festivals

On the mainland, the priests had built more than 11,000 churches and convents.

They were perceptive in realizing their task of "converting" the Indian to their form of Christianity. Saints often could substitute for the ancient gods. Saint's Days and festivals could substitute for pagan rites. Add the Mexican fiesta and it might be possible for the oppressed people to blow off much of their built-up steam.

Every village came to have at least one fiesta a year, according to its patron saint. The Tehuantepecs built up to 25 festivals a year. Where the Aztecs had given 7 or 8 days to feasting and dancing to celebrate ripening of the corn, the church found more discreet ways to give a Christian "look" to the happenings. And, Mardi Gras, at the start of the Lenten season, is celebrated only 4 days.

Half the Aztec time, historians believe, was spent in religious observance. If the Indians were to be kept in a form of slavery, this "release" could not be overlooked.

---

*Most of the fruits and nuts of the Californias were first planted by the friars. However, do not hold them responsible for all the nuts in Hollywood today.

Slowly, the church saints replaced the ancient gods.

And the basic dances and pageantry, native to each tribe, became absorbed into the church-sponsored celebrations. The fiesta, by whatever name, became a break in the life of misery.

Souls exploded like firecrackers. Picturesque, grotesque, the fiesta became a time to ring bells, sing, dance, feast, make noise and get just a little drunk.

A bull fight or a cockfight might help some, too.

Local legend blended with religious ritual and Spanish or Mexican national history to make up the drama of the pageants and the dances. And the native dress, tribe to tribe, added to the color.

The Aztec resignation to death — and its sacrificial glorification — gives today's Mexican a stoic viewpoint on Life's insecurities. The Day of the Dead, with candy skulls for kids, is an example of their viewpoint. The Mexican is ever fascinated with the macabre.

Perhaps, when you live with Death amidst oppression and poverty, the generations season one's soul to laugh at it.

Twenty-Five Steps to Alta California

In October, 1697, the first Mission — and colony — was established at Loreto, about 150 miles north of La Paz.

Financed by wealthy friends, Father Juan María Salvatierra was the spiritual and physical leader of the little group that was to set up this first white settlement in all the Californias.

Loreto was also the first civil capital, and for 132 years the most important town in Baja. But it was never a self-supporting agricultural community. This was another of the unsolvable problems of the missions: they had to depend on the mainland for most of their food and had little or nothing to trade in return.

Two years later, a few miles inland at San Francisco Xavier Vigge-Biaundo, a second mission was founded. Land cultivation

The Path of the Missions and Mission Stations in Baja

Founding Dates, Sequence, and Current Condition

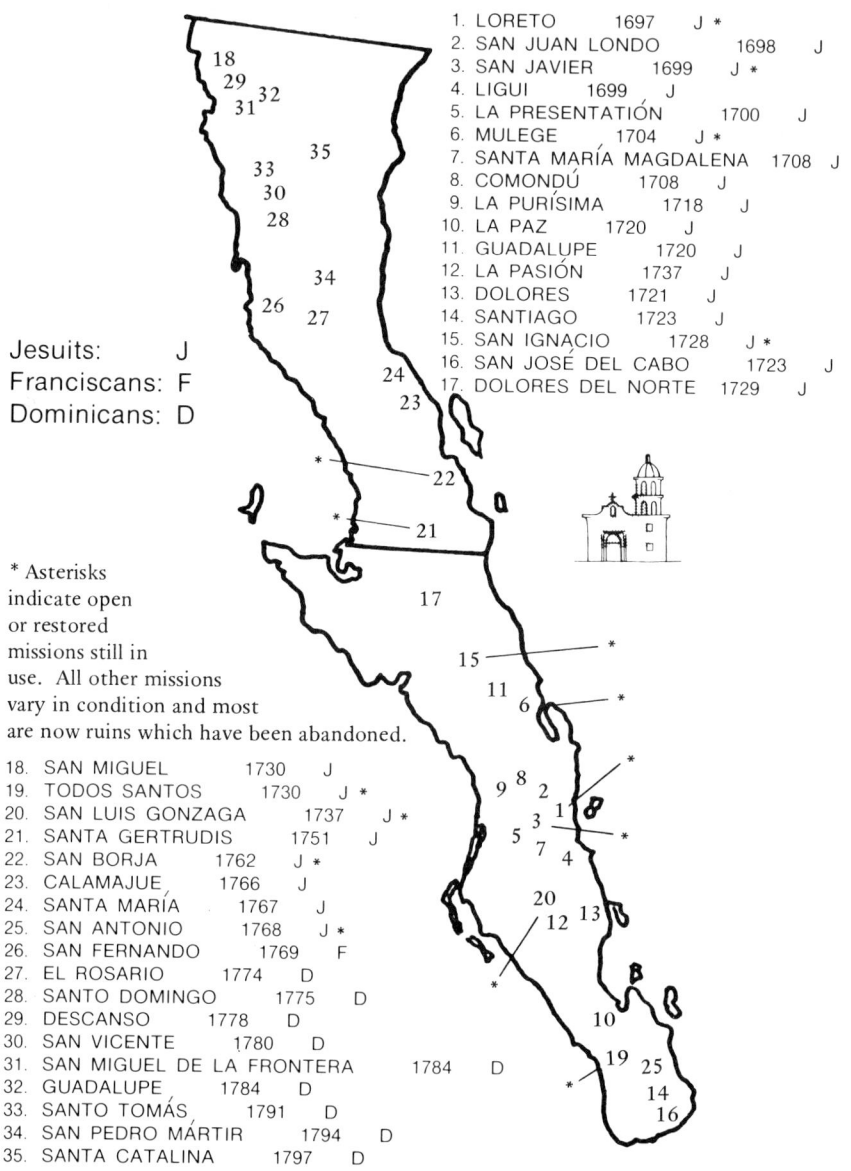

1. LORETO	1697	J *
2. SAN JUAN LONDO	1698	J
3. SAN JAVIER	1699	J *
4. LIGUI	1699	J
5. LA PRESENTATIÓN	1700	J
6. MULEGE	1704	J *
7. SANTA MARÍA MAGDALENA	1708	J
8. COMONDÚ	1708	J
9. LA PURÍSIMA	1718	J
10. LA PAZ	1720	J
11. GUADALUPE	1720	J
12. LA PASIÓN	1737	J
13. DOLORES	1721	J
14. SANTIAGO	1723	J
15. SAN IGNACIO	1728	J *
16. SAN JOSÉ DEL CABO	1723	J
17. DOLORES DEL NORTE	1729	J

Jesuits: J
Franciscans: F
Dominicans: D

* Asterisks indicate open or restored missions still in use. All other missions vary in condition and most are now ruins which have been abandoned.

18. SAN MIGUEL	1730	J
19. TODOS SANTOS	1730	J *
20. SAN LUIS GONZAGA	1737	J *
21. SANTA GERTRUDIS	1751	J
22. SAN BORJA	1762	J *
23. CALAMAJUE	1766	J
24. SANTA MARÍA	1767	J
25. SAN ANTONIO	1768	J *
26. SAN FERNANDO	1769	F
27. EL ROSARIO	1774	D
28. SANTO DOMINGO	1775	D
29. DESCANSO	1778	D
30. SAN VICENTE	1780	D
31. SAN MIGUEL DE LA FRONTERA	1784	D
32. GUADALUPE	1784	D
33. SANTO TOMÁS	1791	D
34. SAN PEDRO MÁRTIR	1794	D
35. SANTA CATALINA	1797	D

Above: Ranchers from hundreds of miles away come to San Javier (22 miles west of Loreto) on Dec. 3 to celebrate the Saint's day. This beautiful mission is one of the most notable built by the Jesuits in Baja California.

Right: San Borja Mission. The bell tower was never completed and the original bells were recently stolen. Less than 10 inhabitants live near this mission now.

Ray Haller

SAN JAVIER'S BELL TOWER OFFERS VIEW OF "MAIN STREET"

This is truly one of the most beautiful missions in all of Baja California. Homes of the local residents line both sides of the wide street, and the rugged natural background creates a most impressive setting. Perhaps because of its comparative isolation in earlier years, San Javier remains in better condition than many other missions which were located on the main routes of travel.

was started, and the first attempt was made to raise livestock. Results were poor, but the need for agricultural land set the pattern for the other missions that were to be established throughout the peninsula.

The first school and hospital in the Californias was established with the mission at San Xavier.

The last Jesuit mission was established in 1767. It was the Mission Santa María, and its brief existence emphasizes the tragedy of the missionaries.

The Ruins of Santa María

It is when you see the ruins of the Jesuit's last, the Mission Santa María — in a desolate, almost unreachable arroyo — that you realize what a heart-breaking task the padres faced.

Maybe I have become something of an agnostic in my older years — and I never was a Catholic — but I bow my head and maybe attempt an erratic gesture of the cross as I view the crumbled adobe walls, the crumbled faith and hopes and dreams of the Mission Santa María.

Santa María, strange and curious, is the most difficult of all missions to reach by land. If you take the faint trail that leads off the main road at Rancho Santa Ynez, you soon find yourself jumping from boulder to boulder down the side of a precipitous mountain, ending up finally with a sudden lurch at the bottom of a gorge.

The scenery is spectacular, if you have time to look at it.

The sides of the gorge rise upward, a scarce fifty feet apart. Their white boulders reflect in a string of clear pools along the bottom of the canyon. Occasional clusters of old palms — planted by the padres themselves — blow and beckon with a shade that might be welcome.

The canyon now opens out into a broader arroyo after a mile or two. You follow this, then the trail turns sharply to the right. It passes between gate-like boulders, then — very unexpectedly — you see for the first time the roofless ruins of this ancient Jesuit

Arturo Pichardo

This is the mission of Santa Rosalía de Mulegé. It was founded in 1705, but the present mission church was built in 1766 by the Jesuit missionary Escalante; the mission has since been repaired and remodeled several times. Just to the right of the mission and slightly below this level is the dam which forms a small lake; it stores the irrigation water for Mulegé's residents. Groves of date palms are located above and below the mission site, creating an impression of a semi-tropical paradise. Many kinds of fruits and vegetables are grown at Mulegé, and in recent years it has also become an increasingly popular destination for sportsmen. If you refer to the map at the beginning of this chapter, you will see the approximate locations and founding dates of the missions established by the Jesuits, Franciscans, and Dominicans. Many of the missions are now in ruins; some have been repaired and restored and are currently in use. Regardless of their present condition, all played their part in the fascinating history of this remarkable peninsula.

mission of Santa María.

It is a sight to tumble your mind, to jar your emotions, backward, backward in time. What was it that brought the Jesuits up this long, barren peninsula and, finally, down this desolate canyon to build this lone, last mission? Why this, the last, before the King would banish them from all Baja and all Spain?

Jesuits Out, Franciscans In

Back in Spain, the King had decreed that all Jesuits be deported from Baja — on penalty of death.

In 1767, came a new governor, Capt. Gaspar de Portola. Out went the Jesuits leaving their 70 years and 25 missions behind. Perhaps 8 or 9 had already been abandoned, even then.

In came the Franciscans, headed by Fra Junipero Serra.

Both Portola and Serra were to play historic roles in that Alta California to the North. Together, in 1768, they set out from Loreto with the Sword and the Cross.

The 25th and last outpost established by the Jesuits had been the ill fated Mission Santa María.

After many weeks, the Portola-Serra expedition passed this point, and made camp at a spot twenty leagues (about 60 miles) northward.

This was destined to be the Mission of San Fernando de Velicata, the 26th mission in Baja, the only one built by the Franciscans. On the map, you can find it about 42 miles south of what is today El Rosario. In fact, you can drive there today, to see what is left of it.

There are a few lonely graves. The outlines of an irrigation ditch. A square stone cistern. Silent. Silent, in a tiny green oasis that once supported sheep, cattle and 530 registered "converts". And always the rocky, cactus-covered mountains to watch over the remains.

Sherilyn Mentes

CONTRASTS IN MISSION PRESERVATION

Mission San Ignacio is located on one side of the town plaza, and is virtually surrounded by a huge grove of date palms. This mission church is one of the best-preserved of the peninsula and is in daily use. Below: The ruins of La Presentación, 34 miles west of Loreto, offer a stark contrast to San Ignacio. It may have been planned as a mission or visita, but today only these ruins remain.

Mike McMahan

The Franciscans Forget Baja

It had been a brave start, but even the Franciscans were to leave this mission — and all Baja — to the Dominican brotherhood in 1773, by a clever compact.* The Dominicans agreed to the responsibility of all Baja missions and, in the end, they added nine more missions there to complete the step-by-step chain started by the Jesuits.

Score: Jesuits 25, Franciscans 1, Dominicans 9.

Meanwhile, the Franciscans found responsibility enough in Alta California. Portola and Fra Serra had moved forward, after founding San Fernando de Velicata, to lay the foundations for Mission San Diego . . . now California. U.S.A.

The Indians Kill A Priest

One of the early Jesuit priests had been killed by the Pericue Indians. His church, San José del Cabo, carries a mural memorial

Ray Haller

Mural above entrance depicts murder of Jesuit priest.

of the bloody event. At least one other died from insurrection. And 15 were left behind in their graves, worn out.

---

*The Dominicans didn't know it but they were left holding the bag, as we say in snipe hunting.

Among the three church orders, there obviously were many men unequal to the fight with Baja. It took more sweat than prayers to get water from this land. And, without water, there could be no mission, no man to survive.

Baja was a tough nut to crack. The Indians were not used to clothes, work or religion. They were loose in their morals. No words for "to marry" existed in their dialects, the priests reported. A woman might wear short hemp apron "curtains" fore and aft, but no more. She also was apt to sleep with the most likely male who happened to be tooling around her neighborhood at nightfall. The priests reported this with some shock and surprise. They added, with equal shock and surprise, that the Indians appeared to have no jealousy in the matter. Without jealousy — that useful support for our modern marriage institution — the priest's "wedding ceremonies" were somewhat less than meaningful. For the bride went her way, the groom his, with any nuptials up for grabs.

It was not surprising that the soldier's syphilis was soon to affect almost the total native population among some tribes. The Cochimi, in central northern Baja, were to be virtually wiped out in a few generations. In 1697, there were 75,000. By 1847, virtually none were left. At Santa Getrudis, five epidemics in 35 years cut the population from 1,700 to 300.

Aschmann quotes sources to suggest, contrariwise, this may have been due to "the system of physical, mental, and moral slavery maintained by the missionaries." Even so, the high incidence of syphilis-caused abortions decimated each generation further. There was simply no time for the Indians to build immunity against the European-introduced diseases.

The Father Who Fathered a Village

One Dominican father, Gabriel Gonzalez, years later, used his own techniques to help stop the falling birth-rate. Today, the village of Todos Santos, in large part, claims him as a progenitor, says Peter Gerhard. It was a good try. But Army records also show that "Father" Gonzalez — as he was affectionately called — made frequent trips to the Army base to obtain "treatment for a venereal disease."

On the mainland, in 1721, a priest was accused of raping 56 women 126 times. One woman resisted and reported it to the bishop. Result: the priest was confined to quarters . . .

The natives lived in small groups or tribes, which the Spanish called *rancherías*. The word did not mean *ranch* or *ranching*, but later was adapted in Alta California to mean *native village.* And, today, it means a *crude country shack,* often nothing more than a brush lean-to thrown up as a temporary shelter from the Baja sun.

The early natives, the padres discovered, didn't even bother to build a lean-to. Sometimes they lived in the shade of a desert shrub, sometimes they found a cave in winter for mutual, tribal warmth for their nakedness.

The natives did most of the labor at the missions — very much against their natural inclinations — in return for food, clothing and trinkets.

The problems never ended for the priests. The gold that Spain had dreamed of was still 80 years from discovery in that new land to the north. But that would be an other California. Another country. Another story.

Pot of Gold in a Mission Wall

Fate had played some incredible jests along the way.

Fortunes had been squandered in trying to conquer, to convert, to colonize Baja.

One of the famous families of history that got its name woven into the tapestry was the house of Borgia. Lucrezia's cousin, María, was to finance three of the missions in Baja, while she was mistress of a Spanish soldier whose other devout aim was to help these Jesuit missionaries.

San Francisco de Borja (the Spanish spelling of the name) was the name given the first mission. Then Mission Calamyget or Calamajué, and finally, Santa María, named for this Borgia duchess herself.

And perhaps it was the curse of the Borgias that helped bring still another ruination to the missions. It was in the spring of 1900 that a wandering goatherd camped for the night in the shadow of the wall of this ill-fated church, Santa María.

Next morning, the sun lit up the base of the wall where previous rains had washed away the dirt. The herdsman looked: that protrusion, it looked like an old earthenware pot . . . Quickly he dug it out . . .

Santa María! More than $6,000 in gold tumbled out of the pot!

It is easy to figure what would happen. The story spread. No matter if it weren't all true, it got bigger with every re-telling. From Santa María back to Loreto, the walls of the missions were ripped apart by vandals. For nothing. Time and nature — and a crazy story — were in league to complete the destruction.

By the 1930s, when Mexico destroyed the power of the church, the missions of Baja were already a shambles, only a few holding promise for restoration.

Baja had won. Baja had defeated even God Himself.

MISSION RUINS AT SAN FERNANDO
This was the only mission founded by the Franciscans in Baja California. Note the graves in the foreground; at one time the mission had about 1,500 Indians but now only these crumbling adobe walls and the remains of the old irrigation ditches testify to the importance which San Fernando once enjoyed.

Pirates & People:

Strange Characters
of Baja

13. *The Buccaneers of Baja*
Cavendish, the British Pirate
The Revolutionary Mr. Walker
What's in a Name "Ho-Nez . . . "
Mi Amigo, Richard Daggett
The Russians Colonize Baja
The Americans Trick the British

There's a crazy-quilt in my mind as I look back on all those trips to Baja.

Fact and fiction overlap in the montage of the years. Old friends, chance acquaintances, legendary characters all are there, woven into the warp and woof of the rich tapestry, tiled in the soft colors of the mosaic, standing up to lean over my shoulder and make certain this narrative forgets them not.

So, with one hand raised in Boy Scout's honor and the other quietly crossing two fingers behind my back, let me try to sort them out.

Pirates flourished there in Baja at one time. And what a reckless bunch of freebooters they were. They didn't have it as glamorous — if history runs true — as Jean Lafitte and Henry Morgan and Captain Kidd in the Gulf and Caribbean waters. But we have a hunch they must have had more than their share of nerve, Baja being the tyrant it is.

Morgan once ventured there. He is reputed to have assaulted one Spanish vessel carrying the "treasures of Baja" off the coast of Panama. This would have to have been a cargo of pearls from La Paz and maybe a few wild animal skins. Only a few Spanish ships carried gold and silver in these waters. Morgan must have been disappointed after his earlier treasures from Mexico and South America.

Most of the Baja pirates were English or Dutch, of course. This was Spanish land. And enemy governments gave tacit encouragement to pirate tactics in their continuing attrition against Spain for the new domains.

Cavendish, the British Pirate

It was the British pirate, Tom Cavendish, who came off with a great pirate victory when he captured the Manila galleon, *Santa Ana*, as she approached the Tip of Baja near Cabo San Lucas, on Nov. 4, 1587. The Santa Ana was riding deep in the water; her treasure included gold, pearls, and rich silks, along with many other items of great value to Mexico. It was later determined that the cargo represented an original investment at Manila of more than 1,000,000 pesos, with a sale value of more than twice that amount — had it ever reached its intended destination. Cavendish's exploit set off wild stories on the possibilities for profitable buccaneering.

You can imagine many a Dutch or British trading ship was intrigued with the idea of running up, at least temporarily, a black flag with skull-and-crossbones. Even the French might be encouraged to think this would be good sport and in the "national interest", as the politicians now say.

The pirate era was in. Both sides of the peninsula hide a succession of sheltered coves, *ensenadas* (like the upper peninsula town of that same name), and it was easy enough for the freebooters to lie in wait for passing ships.

But the Spanish weren't behind doors when brains were handed out. To protect themselves, they started sailing out a naval convoy, "armed to the teeth".*

---

*So-called, because of the pirates' edgy habit of carrying a dagger clenched between their molars.

A fleet or *flota* of a dozen armed ships then became an *armada* to protect and convoy one treasure ship. Since the treasure in earlier experiences carried gold and silver, the name was applied to the Spanish convoy: *flota plata* (silver fleet).

The Manila "Plate Fleet"

The Mexican plate fleet sailed from Acapulco, Manzanillo, or other mainland ports past the tip of Baja to ride that equatorial current across the Pacific to the Philippines. Hence the name became "Manila plate fleet". It must have been a fabulous and beautiful sight — certainly never fully pictured even in Hollywood epics — as the dozen ships pushed forth in close formation under full sail.

Perhaps they might veer right up the California coasts before turning into the sunset. If a pirate hove in sight there were bays, too, in which they might hide or make repairs.

The Spanish knew these coasts and had the best maps then extant for their galleon pilots. The explorer Sebastian Vizcaíno (Vizcaino Bay — and the accursed Malarrimo, remember?) had explored the perimeters of the peninsula from 1596 to 1603 and his charts provided a considerable advantage in this game of hide-and-seek.

So the Spanish won this phase of the contest and the English, Dutch and French pirates had only minor successes for the next century and a half.

Frankly, there wasn't too much to rob.

But finally, on Dec. 22, 1709, the British privateer Woodes Rogers surprised a galleon off the tip of the peninsula and captured it with ease. The prize was the *Nuestra Señora de la Encarnación y Desengaño;* her commander's lack of skill was later determined to have caused the loss of the galleon. When prisoners from the *Encarnación* were questioned, it was learned that a larger ship named the *Begoña* had left Manila in company with the captured galleon. When Rogers intercepted it a few days later, his three ships were badly damaged by the guns of the *Begoña* and were in danger of sinking. The English ships had been unable to inflict significant damage on the galleon, and Rogers was forced to withdraw in defeat.

Ray Haller

FEDERAL PRISON AT MULEGE

With the pirates gone and almost forgotten, one has to look hard to find a potential criminal in most of Baja — there are problems in the border towns at times — but many "crimes" of the people who live in Baja could be most honestly called "crimes of passion." I'd guess that jealousy resulting from the "triangle" would account for a good many of the inmates in this pleasantly-whitewashed prison. The men here rarely try to escape, for they are allowed considerable freedom and may work for wages if they can obtain local employment.

So despite their occasional successes, the pirates were actually a bust in Baja. Like the conquistadores and the padres, they had to learn the hard way that it's very difficult to make a living from this arid land — and even harder to achieve fame or fortune in the sea around it.

New Orleans may pay a certain obeisance to its pirates on Mardi Gras, but Baja dismisses the whole subject with a yawn. Only one word remains:

Pichilingues is the Baja word for pirates (I find it nowhere else in the Spanish speaking world). But — argue others — the origin may be Dutch, and *pichilingue* may be a corruption of the Flemish place name, *Vlissingen,* from which the Dutch freebooters came. After all, the Dutch have always been traders in pearls, so *Pichilingues* probably was their hangout near La Paz.

At any rate, the word itself is dying along with the bloodthirsty legends themselves. Only one place does it linger on: today *Pichilingues* is the name of your Mazatlán-to-La Paz ferry landing in Baja. Welcome: pirates came before you . . .

— But you'll find no pirates now. No. Maybe they can be found in today's bordertown Tijuana. But not in La Paz.

The Revolutionary Mr. Walker

Tijuana has been the storybook plotting ground for revolution, filibusters, political take-overs and piratical dreams. And yet the peninsula actually was free of most of the Latin American revolutionary action and overthrow that was a part of this century's early years on Mexico's mainland.

Just the same — there was *one* war. And it was a doozy! There was one man, who had one dream: to take over Baja for his own empire. Here, believe it or not, was an American trying to "confiscate" the entire peninsula.

Colonel William Walker was what was called in the mid-1800's a "filibusterer", a word sometimes also applied to pirates. As a matter of fact, even as the English and Dutch and French encouraged a pirate here and there, so did the United States, let us say, *not* discourage the private armed expeditions of

Americans, inspired under the new Monroe Doctrine to be ambitious with armed expeditions into more of the Western Hemisphere.

If such a filibusterer succeeded, he was a hero. If he failed, he ended his life in disgrace.*

Colonel Walker's aim was Baja. His army had been secretly recruited in San Francisco and, for weeks he had been below the border, hiding in the mountains, marching through the desert and fighting against small bands of Mexicans somehow unwilling to be "liberated".

The filibusterer's forays went on for weeks, amidst unending rumors. Then, in May, 1854, Walker sent a message to the U.S. Army in San Diego, demanding a meeting at the Tijuana border.

San Diego was only 17 miles away, and the San Diegans had heard the rumors and were anxious to see the confrontation. They came by buggy, wagon and horseback.

It was a chance to watch a battle! They perched high on the hill on the American side where they could see the scene about to be enacted down below them at the border.

Captain H. S. Burton and Major J. McKinstry of the U.S. Cavalry were known to head the Americans. Colonel Walker was thought to be camped in the nearby Hacienda de Tia Juana (near what is now the Caliente Race Track).

The crowd was impatient, curious and as full of rumors as a boot camp at shipping time.

At long last the revolutionaries appeared.

There was Colonel William Walker, drawn up to his full 5-foot height, muscles tensed like springs in his 100-pound body, attired in ragged boots, torn trousers, short jacket with most of the brass buttons missing. On top of his head perched a ridiculously high-crowned white beaver hat, soiled — but Walker was still proud.

*And abruptly.

Only 34 of Walker's 300-man "army" tagged with him. They were even more ragged, surely as hungry-looking as the colonel himself. Slowly, with a certain dignity, they marched across to safety in the United States.

"I am Col. William Walker, late president of Sonora." The little man inched himself up to 5' 1". "I wish to surrender my force to the United States."

The war was over. It was the sad end to a flamboyant dream. The people may have laughed — but History was not laughing at this little Napoleon. Two years later, Col. Walker won a new reputation as a "great and successful American filibusterer" all over Central America. He even conquered Nicaragua.*

Yes, Col. Walker finally made it. But not in Baja. Baja had defeated the little American filibusterer — just as it had the other pirates, the conquistadores and the padres. Baja had won.

Maps are the Tombstones of History

The story of any country is revealed in names. Man's pride in his name spatters any map. Especially when others honor him for good deeds along the frontier land. In the United States, honored names extend from Washington to Boonesboro to Sutter's Mill. The right man ... in the right place ... at the right time in History ...

Dallas was a man. And Houston. And Laramie. Few of us now can find new frontiers on which to write our names, except amidst the graffiti at the gas station.

In Baja, the padres passed out most of the early names and the saints were first with the honors, depending on which saint's day a new mission was founded. San Diego, Santa Monica, Santa Rosa and San Francisco carried on this concept through Upper California. Los Angeles, however, was named the City of the Angels, prophetically looking forward to the population's decimation on today's freeways.

---

*In San José, Costa Rica, there stands today a marble statue to Walker — but depicting him as being driven off by the Central American republics. Honduras eventually stood him in front of a firing squad.

The explorers of Baja came in a poor second to the saints. Only recent cartographers use the romantic names for the Gulf of California: "The Sea of Cortez". Vizcaíno was given the bay and the arid desert on the western side.*

A quondam Aunt Jane translated as Tia Juana and usage shortened this to *Tijuana.* But most of the names on my map easily trace to the day of the year the founding Father trudged be-sandaled feet onto the sand, crossed himself for God first, Spain second, and the saint, third.

Look at the map for San Matías, San Marcos, San Lucas, San Juan. That's right — the four apostles: Matthew, Mark, Luke and John. Look at the distaff side: Santa Rosalía, Santa Anita, Santa Catarina, Santa Gertrudis, Santa Rita . . . And many more. It was a gracious custom. Be humble on these hallowed grounds.

"What's in a Name? . . . Ho-Nez"

Family names in Baja are always intriguing to trace.

On one of my early trips my then faulty Spanish was baffled during an introduction to "Señor Ho'nez" — as I caught the name pronounced.

"Con mucho gusto!" I replied in my best phrasebook language for introductory politeness. Meanwhile, my brain was step-by-stepping a slow process: a "j" is pronounced "h" in Spanish. So . . . Sure enough, I realized as he later wrote out his name for me: It was *Jones.*

He was third-generation *Bajacalifornio,* a *mestizo's* mixture of American and Indian and Spanish bloods. His grandfather was an early Stateside adventurer in Baja, settled in this new land.

You'll find *"Dah'veez"* — Davis — and *"Smeeth"* — Smith — along with descendants of many other gringo forebears with familiar family names. And, curiously enough, they speak *only Spanish. Si!* So the pronunciation is different . . . after all, what's in a name?

---

*No saint in his right mind would have wanted that desert named after him.

Mi Amigo, Richard Daggett

I remember Richard Daggett, a wonderful old character I met a quarter of a century ago at Bahia de Los Angeles. He was then in his fifties, but his mind was sharp as a cactus needle as he helped me piece together some fascinating background material.

The original Daggett in Baja — his father — was a junior officer on a German ship that touched port at that bay with a cargo of bricks for an inland mine, in the 1880s.

DICK DAGGETT GIVES US SOME ROAD INFORMATION

Although this photograph was taken many years ago, it shows Dick with wrench in hand and that's how I remember him. He could fix almost anything, and he helped many a gringo get going again, after Baja's "roads" had tortured a vehicle until it was stopped cold. Whenever word reached him at his home at the Bay of Los Angeles that a traveler was stranded, he'd throw whatever he felt was needed into a truck and come to the rescue — at any hour of the day or night. A truly remarkable man who, so far as I know, never charged any American as much as he would have had to pay for similar repairs in the United States, though he was well aware of U.S. prices and could easily have charged even more.

The sailor hated the ship, the cargo and the captain especially.

He jumped ship.

THERE IT IS: BAJA!

The German captain was furious. He instituted an extensive search, aided — but misdirected — by the Mexicans who knew where Daggett was hiding all the time. Finally, disgusted, the German captain sailed away and left him to Baja.

Daggett got a job in the mine, married a pretty senorita from San Ignacio, and today the grandchildren and great-grandchildren of the old fugitive German seaman may include the "native" who creates that turtle steak for you or helps you beach your boat.

What's in a name? Echoes of adventurous days gone by. Ubiquitous shoes and ships and sealing wax — and bloods that mix and merge in wonderous ways on new frontiers . . .

The Russians Try to Colonize Baja

There are about twenty Russian family names you might encounter in the area of Guadalupe, about 50 miles south of Tecate. But their faces look Mexican and, except for the very old ones, they speak only Spanish.

I have found two old samovars in Guadalupe but today they are only curious ornaments to the villagers.

Once, the Russians tried to colonize Baja early in this century. Three generations have erased almost every trace. Today, no Russian church, no gravestones in foreign language to hallow a memory or stir up a witch hunt from a northern neighbor. The Russians were escaping the tyranny of a czar and the impending Bolshevik Revolution — and were all too ready to forget all that heritage, that past.

It was just as well. Baja mixes a batter from whatever comes and the ingredients all blend into today's bread. Only the names remain — faint memories of the empty bottles on the spice rack.*

It was hardly the same in the States. The colonists in the United States long held first to their national identities: the Germans in St. Louis, the French in New Orleans, the Polish in Chicago, the Scandinavians in Minnesota . . .

---

*A little anise often goes well with the pepper.

But not in Baja. Many attempts were made to "colonize" Baja, but Baja always won. So samovars are simply nice to look at. You can't make *café con leche* in a samovar.

The Other Nationalities Try

The Spanish were the first to colonize and blend with the Indians to make Mexicans. The Americans and the British came with too little and too late to have a dominant influence. The Italians and the French blended with only a trace.

Baja's colonization boom of the 1880s was probably an overflow from the extraordinary land promotions northward in San Diego and Los Angeles.

The International Company of Mexico advertised at that time that it controlled 18-million acres of Baja land (mostly in the northern sector).

And millions in American dollars and British pounds were to go down the peninsula drain. Colonies came, did their best and either disappeared or were absorbed into the batter.

The arid climate and the lack of water were too much for the agricultural future then promised. The Americans attempted to colonize the broad valley some 125 miles south of Ensenada (named on some maps as the Santa María Plains). But only the searing sun greeted their efforts, year after year. At last the colony disappeared — many of the colonists returning to the States. The next year, natives say, came the biggest winter rainfall in all Baja memory . . . ah! here was another of Baja's tricks!

And always, there are tricksters to out-trick the trickiest.

The Americans Trick the British

When the next spring came to the valley, it was aglow with wild flowers. The cacti put forth their vivid blossoms of red and yellow; the century plants grew high with their once-in-a-lifetime regal crown of blooms.

It must have been a land promoter's dream to behold. I've seen it after even a lesser winter rainfall and it is breath-taking.

This is how the wheat mill at San Quintín looked many years ago when we photographed the site. It has since been torn down.

The Americans, no dummies, brought the British in for a look. They jumped at the bait. So British colonization took over where the Americans had failed.

But spring in Baja arrives early and leaves the same way. The British soon discovered the fraud. But, with Anglo-Saxon reserve, they went ahead with their plans, quietly, figuring that one good fraud deserves another.

To give the appearance of truth to their claims for the valley's productivity the British began to build a flour mill at San Quintín to process all the wheat that was to be grown on these fertile fields.

The entire mill had to be constructed with imported materials, of course. And to entice the next crop of suckers it was put into operation . . . with *imported wheat* . . .

So the land was sold again. At necessarily-reduced prices. And most of the people who bought were now *Bajacalifornios*.

Perhaps they knew that the wheat mill was a fraud, but also they knew the land was not.

With Mexican ingenuity, the new native owners looked for a new source of water and found it — in the upside-down rivers and underground springs beneath their lands.

Today, this broad valley of Santa María is filled with ranches and gardens producing tomatoes, lettuce, radishes, and lots and lots of Mexican peppers.

And, yes . . . a little bit of wheat . . .

So now, unfortunately, it's time to sum it all up as best I can. And though the Baja of tomorrow will be much tamer than the one I've loved all these years, I'll never get over that irresistible urge to return. Maybe I took a few chances I shouldn't have, like fishing off the tip in a very small boat, or digging out the torpedo shown above from it's hiding place on the beach at Malarrimo. Some of Baja's unluckier travelers — including a few Americans — have lost their lives in accidents while driving on the primitive roads of my memorable Baja; the cross beside the road along Concepción Bay testifies that somebody went over the side here. But I'm going back for more of Baja's enriching experiences, and I hope you will too, as we examine the Baja of today and tomorrow in the final chapter.

Personal Observations:

25 Years
a Baja
Aficionado

14. *"Wetbacks": Millionaire Smugglers at Work*
The Tempting World of Tourist Money
Peyote vs. Bourbon
A New Geothermal Field
Farmers and the State of the Onion
The Irresistible Urge to Return

In 1970, the AP reported that the U.S. Border Patrol had arrested a total of 63,933 "deportable aliens" just north of the Baja border in California during the preceding year.

"Some smugglers take 30 aliens at a time," U.S. Attorney Harry Seward said. He estimated a smuggler might make a million dollars a year in that risky business.

The smuggled, most often, are the poor Mexicans of Baja, lured by better-paying jobs on farms and in California's hotels, restaurants and homes. After they earn a little, they generally head back to Baja where the dollars are exchanged for pesos, which go a little farther than in the States.

"Wetbacks" they call them — from the equivalent problem in Texas where they swim the Rio Grande. But there's no river crossing here and it's possible to walk across many places along the 200-mile strip in spite of radar and plane patrols.

After all, the "wetbacks" make invaluable hand laborers during the harvest season and there are across-the-border interests that obviously don't want to change the status quo, at least for this seasonal flow back-and-forth.

The flow of Americans the other way, the race-trackers, the bull-fight aficionados, the day-tourists have only a verbal statement to make as they breeze by for a bordertown visit.

Tijuana and Mexicali had become boomtowns when America mistakenly went *Dry* in 1919, and they later lost much of the tourist traffic and revenue when we went *Wet* again in 1933 — which was about the time something else significant was happening all over Mexico.

The Mexican farmers wanted back their own farm lands. Big American holdings all over Mexico were "expropriated" by President Lazaro Cardenas. Some of the big farms below Mexicali in the rich lower Colorado River basin were taken over from the Americans by squatters.

Many displaced laborers have become seasonal "wetbacks" while others discarded farming for the higher wages (the highest in all Mexico) available in Tijuana.

But all of this upheaval, instability, and economic pressure only seems to perpetuate and reinforce the determination of Baja's citizenry to succeed. Slowly, surely, a new pattern has begun to emerge.

The Tempting World of Tourist Money

More than $100,000,000 will be invested in Baja California during the 'Seventies. The aim: Touri$m.

Tourist dollars have been a mainstay of Mexico's economy on the mainland, with Acapulco now developed as one of the world's better resorts and Mexico City growing fabulously in popularity since the Olympics.

Northern Baja (the top half of the peninsula) has been one of Mexico's 29 states for the last twenty years and is expected to continue to move ahead with exceptional strides. The southern half, still a "territory" — in spite of the fact that Sunset magazine keeps reversing the two designations — may yet fulfill the "impossible dream" of Cortés in other golden ways.

The Mexican National Tourist Council has a five-year plan in work that is committing $75,000,000 to the development of the mainland and Baja shorelines around the Sea of Cortez. "Recreation" is the key word in this project. Both government and private capital are at work.

Private capital has announced the building of some 2300 new rooms along the Gulf.

The World Bank and the Inter-American Development Bank are putting up much of this new dough. This is the first time these banks have ear-marked money as a practical investment for tourism. Yes, it's a going business . . . going south of the Border . . .

Peyote vs. Bourbon

Peyote comes from the Mexican cactus, mescal, and has been around for several centuries. The Aztecs reputedly discovered it first.*

Baja Indians used peyote in "religious" rites for the wonderful, colorful "visions" the shriveled brown buttons produced. The active ingredient in peyote is alkaloid mescaline (LSD is a synthetic comparative).

In this particular cactus, the mescaline accumulates in the center and it is brought to market (many markets in Baja have it) as a fibrous, brown, dessicated substance that someone from the Old South might compare to a dried tobacco stalk, the "poor man's 'baccy".

The effects of peyote I report by hearsay, since one of my bourbon-drinking friends from the Old South decided to experiment. Report: first you get the cold shivers, giddiness, numbness and a painful sensitivity to bright light. You have to endure the miseries of poison before you get the intoxication of the dreams to come.

*They also invented pulque and 400 gods of drink.

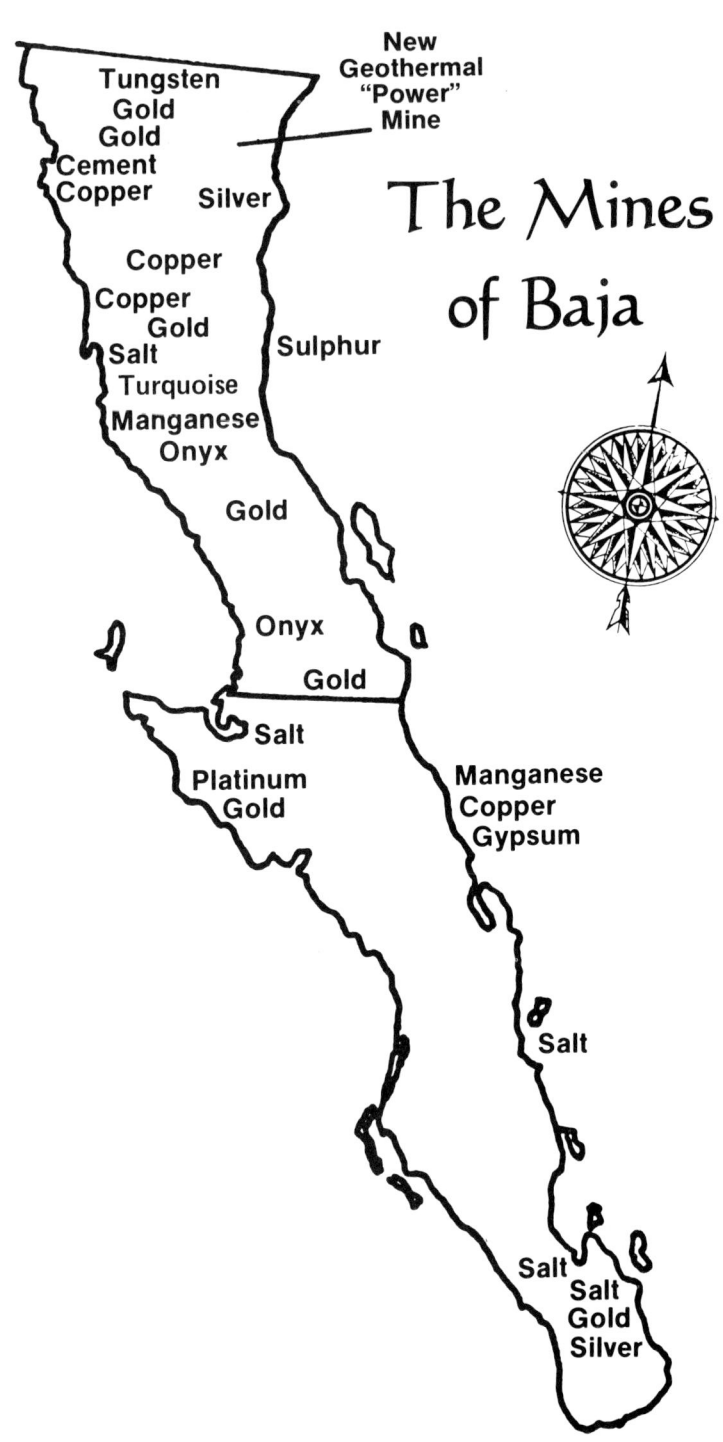

In other words, the hangover comes first.

He said that heavy use could give you the equivalent of the D.T.'s. The legs give way. Your yawns become spasms, your chest aches and a "boundless, crushing melancholy overcomes your soul". End of report.*

A New Geothermal Field

Although the history of mining in Baja California is fascinating, we haven't enough space here to explore its many facets. But on the accompanying map you'll find the general locations indicated for many of the minerals which have contributed to — or detracted from — the fortunes of those who gambled for riches in Baja California. Old shafts and tunnels and the ruins of primitive arrastres are scattered throughout the peninsula. Some were successful; most were not. Even where the finds were promising, sometimes the problem of transporting supplies — and often even water itself — were so great that any realistic point of view could have predicted certain failure. But human nature changes little; today the gamblers among us merely lose their *dinero* more comfortably in air-conditioned casinos.

Yet there is one "mine" in Baja, a modern one, which can be considered a genuine success — with an even more promising future. It will mine for *power*.

Just south of Cerro Prieto, you'll see great white majestic plumes of "smoke" rising toward the sky. Closer, if you turn off the highway, you'll discover that they're really clouds of steam; even closer and you can hear the roaring sound that is coming from the earth itself.

Here's a modern geothermal "mine" which captures Nature's own boiling heat and can convert it into electric power. This is a gamble with very favorable odds; in New Zealand this kind of "mining" has already proved its feasibility.

The United States is watching the project with great interest because it could well be the first step in creating cheap electric power. And maybe the next step in creating desalinated water.

*He went back to Bourbon.

THERE IT IS: BAJA!

Pat McMahan

The new geothermal generating station, powered by hot water from beneath the surface at Cerro Prieto, may already be in operation by the time you read this. The generators are scheduled to produce 75,000 kilowatts. Cerro Prieto is south (and a little east) of Mexicali.

This can be vital to the future of the Imperial Valley on the northern side of the border. Dr. Robert W. Rex, professor of geology at the Institute of Geophysics and Planetary Physics at the University of California at Riverside, is the most interested observer on the scene.

Dr. Rex estimates that the Imperial Valley may be able to "mine" down — perhaps a mile into Mother Earth — and tap the underground heat and water source *below* to provide an electric power yield of 20,000 megawatts (20,000-million watts). Plus distilled water as a byproduct from the steam equal to 3½ million acre-feet. Eventually a potential 10 million acre-feet of water at a cost of less than $10 per acre-foot.*

And all this, mind you, with no pollution to the atmosphere . . .

---

*Comparatively, crude oil in Texas costs $20,000 per acre-foot. Coca-Cola in Atlanta would be $400,000 per acre-foot. And good bourbon in Kentucky would have to be priced around $14,000,000 per acre-foot.

Could be here is the greatest "mine" of all in Baja, a pilot that will change deserts of California and the destinies of generations to come. Perhaps Baja's future as well.

Farmers and the State of the Onion

The outlook for farming in Baja is ever so dependent on that water, too. Irrigation from the Colorado River (after California sponges up most of it) is not enough. The few mountain streams of northern Baja help, but are dependent upon inconsistent rains. The early American and British colonies found that a 7-year-drought could wither the fondest hopes. And Baja's total water table keeps dropping.

Potentially, with regular rains or controlled irrigation, there are thousands of acres of rich valley floor that could become truck gardens. And a whole desert that could be turned into a blooming paradise — or, at minimum, an oasis or two.

Perhaps the geothermal project at Cerro Prieto will be beneficial for us. It may solve Baja's water problem — and ours, too. This section of Mother Earth then might settle back to normalcy, if she could just let off this little steam, once in a while . . .

The Irresistible Urge to Return

Well, we've let off quite a little steam ourselves. If at times we've appeared to be too critical, count it no more than a lover's quarrel. My old mistress keeps calling me back.

She's a puzzle. And peculiar. Often preposterous. Perplexing. Paradoxical! And maybe perfidious. But she's my Baja!

We acknowledge Baja's dream of the future, but we still have mixed emotions when comparing this dream with our memories of earlier years. If we could, I'm sure we'd cling to that magnificent and comparatively primitive peninsula of the past. That just isn't possible; change *will* come.

The long-awaited highway linking the extremities of this amiably arid land of mystery was completed in 1973. But progress has a price. To me, it seems unfortunate that the thousands of new visitors who will explore this incredibly beautiful desert in the years ahead cannot also experience the greater challenge of the truly rugged roads — just two tire tracks really — which formerly restricted travelers to a much slower pace.

Now, even bicyclists are beginning to explore the "tamed" sections which have been paved; *True* magazine recently reported on two such hardy souls who claimed they must have been the first to cycle more than 550 miles in Baja del Sur. Could be, but I wouldn't bet on it.

The new ferry, *Presidente Diaz Ordaz,* links the new highway in Baja with the main highway at Guaymas in mainland Mexico. Guaymas is just a pleasant day's drive from Arizona. Will this constantly increasing tourist pressure endanger Baja's enchanting natural features? We hope not, but the very modifications which allow plants to survive in a desert environment also serve to prevent rapid growth. One thoughtless tourist, axe in hand, can mutilate or destroy — in just a few minutes — a venerable cardón that may be more than a hundred years old. Future visitors entering Baja California will need to be more considerate than some of us have been in the past, if the peninsula's vegetation is to remain as beautiful as it is today.

Many conservationists have expressed concern over the predicted changes in Baja California's natural resources of plants and animals. In the March-April 1970 issue of *Pacific Discovery,* George Lindsay has summarized some of the problems which now exist, and included his suggestions for the peninsula's future. Every person with a sincere interest in Baja will enjoy reading this feature article, *Some Natural Values of Baja California.*

I'm sure my sentiments are clearly understood. But no matter what Baja's future may be, I'll just have to be there sharing it with her — good times or bad. I've loved her far too long, and much too deeply, to ever leave her now. I've studied every source I know about, and I'm sure there are still many beaches and byways that will remain a challenge for years to come with our "La Burrita No. 4." And if I listen to Walter, there'll be a "La Burrita No. 5", maybe complete with his latest invention: an electronic umbrella that reaches out and holds itself over your sleeping bag when it starts to rain.

A couple of my old fishing buddies will be "roughing it" in those new luxury hotels, I'm afraid. Their weak backs can't take the bumpy roads any more. They fly now. Maybe I'll get around to more of that, too.

For when November's cool winds blow in, I've got to be there. At the Tip. The marlin are running! Get the gear ready . . .

April it will have to be the desert, to see what a new Spring has sprung among all those weird, wild blossoms. Look at that century plant break out its regal proclamations of joy, right on its own flag pole! I've gotta get a picture of that one. And then I'll reach over and pick my wild orégano, crush it between my fingers and say,

"What'll we cook tonight, boys?"

In between times, there'll always be my favorite: surf-fishing. Some day I've got to match that 105-pound totuava that Donn landed.

Pat will be skin-diving. The rest of the family, digging Easter clams at San Quintín. Walter will be cleaning a mess of quail and weaving the bacon in the choice breasts for *Quail a la McMahan.* And Tommy. Tommy, 10 ducks trophied around his neck, pushing back his sloppy hat and saying:

"Who's the cook who ordered all these damn' ducks?"

Yes, the future keeps getting mixed up with the past.

There It Is: Baja!

Good Lord, please . . . please don't make me turn in my sleeping bag too soon. I just gotta go, *one more time* . . .

NOTES

NOTES

Suggestions For Further Reading

Used books can sometimes be bought if the title is out of print, although they may be expensive if they are in short supply. Inquire at your local book store; if they cannot help you, try writing to Dawson's Book Shop, 535 Larchmont Blvd., Los Angeles, California 90004.

If you enjoy armchair adventures there are books like North's *Camp & Camino in Lower California* which may be found in most libraries. Even though many books of this type were poorly written, they do reveal the adventures and hardships which early travelers encountered in Baja California. The listing is alphabetical, and includes not only books but a few other kinds of publications.

Here then, are enough suggestions to introduce you to the peninsula and its absorbing history. Happy reading....

Aschmann, Homer. *The Central Desert of Baja California: Demography and Ecology.* Ibero-Americana, No. 42. Berkeley and Los Angeles: University of California. Riverside: Manessier reprint, 1967.

Automobile Club of Southern California. *Baja California Norte, Baja California Sur, Baja California (map).* Los Angeles: 1971.

Baegert, Johann Jakob. *Observations in Lower California.* Berkeley & Los Angeles: University of California Press, 1952.

Bancroft, Griffing. *Lower California, a Cruise; the Flight Least Petrel.* New York: Putnam's Sons, 1932.

Bancroft, Hubert Howe. *History of the North Mexican States and Texas.* San Francisco: The History Co., (2 vols. published as vols. 15-16 of collected works) 1884-1889.

_____. *History of Mexico, Volumes I and II.* San Francisco: The History Company, 1886.

Barrett, Ellen C. *Baja California 1535-1956.* * Los Angeles: Bennett & Marshall, 1957.

_____. *Baja California II.* * Los Angeles: Westernlore Press, 1967.

Blaisdell, Lowell L. *The Desert Revolution: Baja California, 1911.* Madison, Wisconsin: University of Wisconsin Press, 1962.

Bush, Wesley A. *Paradise to Leeward.* New York: Van Nostrand, 1954.

Castillo, Bernal Diaz del. *The Discovery and Conquest of Mexico.* New York: Farrar, Straus.

Chapman, Charles E. *A History of California, The Spanish Period.* New York: The Macmillan Co., 1921.

Clavigero, Francisco Xavier. *The History of (Lower) California.* Translated by Sara E. Lake. Palo Alto: Stanford University Press, 1937. Riverside: Manessier reprint, 1971.

Cleland, Robert Glass. *California Pageant: The Story of Four Centuries.* New York: Alfred A. Knopf, 1955.

Cortes, Hernan. *Letters of Cortes.* New York: G. P. Putnam's Sons, 1908.

Cowan, Robert Ernest, and Cowan, Robert Grannis. *Bibliography of the History of California, 1510-1930.* 3 volumes. San Francisco: John Henry Nash, 1933.

Crow, John. *Mexico Today.* New York: Harper & Row, 1957.

Cudahy, John. *Mañanaland.* New York: Duffield, 1928.

Davidson, Winifred. *Where California Began.* San Diego: McIntyre Publishing Co., 1929.

Dunne, Peter Masten. *Black Robes in California.* Berkeley and Los Angeles: University of California Press, 1952.

Eldredge, Zoeth Skiner, ed. *History of California, Volume I.* New York: Century History Co., ca. 1915.

Engelhardt, Zephyrin. *The Missions and Missionaries of California.* Second edition, volume 1 only. Santa Barbara: 1929.

Gardner, Erle Stanley, *Land of Shorter Shadows.* New York: Morrow, 1948.

_____. *Hunting the Desert Whale.* New York: William Morrow and Co., 1960.

_____. *Hovering Over Baja.* New York: William Morrow & Co., 1961.

_____. *The Hidden Heart of Baja.* New York: William Morrow & Co., 1962.

Gerhard, Peter. *Pirates on the West Coast of New Spain.* Glendale: The Arthur H. Clark Co., 1960.

_____. *Pirates in Baja California.* Tlapalan, Mexico: Editorial Tlilan (printed by G. Yamada) 1963.

Gerhard, Peter, and Gulick, Howard E. *Lower California Guidebook.* Glendale: The Arthur H. Clark Co., (Fourth Edition) 1967.

Hancock, Ralph, with Ray Haller, Mike McMahan, and Frank Alvarado. *Baja California.* "Original trip by authors in 1950." Los Angeles: Academy Publishers, 1953.

Holmes, Brig. Gen. Maurice G. USMC, ret. *Spanish Nautical Explorations Along the Coast of the Californias.* University of Southern California, Thesis, 1959.

Johnson, William W. *Baja California.* Time-Life (The American Wilderness Series) 1973.

Kroeber, Alfred L. "The Seri," *Southwest Museum Papers, VI.* Los Angeles: Southwest Museum, 1931.

Krutch, Joseph Wood. *The Forgotten Peninsula: A Naturalist in Baja California.* New York: William Morrow and Co., 1961.

Leigh, Randolph. *Forgotten Waters.* New York: Lippincott, 1941.

Leopold, Aldo Starker. *Wildlife of Mexico.* Berkeley: University of California Press, 1959.

Lewis, Leland R. *Baja Sea Guide, Vol. II.* San Francisco: Miller Freeman, 1971.

Loftin, Grace, Publisher. *Mexico's West Coast Magazine.* San Ysidro, California: 301 Sycamore Road.

MacNutt, Francis Augustus. *Hernando Cortes and the Conquest of Mexico.* New York: G. P. Putnam's Sons, 1909.

Mardariaga, Salvador de. *Hernan Cortes: The Conqueror of Mexico.* New York: The Macmillan Co., 1941.

Martinez, Pablo L. *A History of Lower California.* Mexico D. F., 1960.

Massey, William C. "Tribes and Languages of Baja California," *Southwestern Journal of Anthropology,* V. (Autumn 1949)

Mateo Manje, Juan. *Luz de Tierra Incognita, 1693-1701: The Journal of Captain Juan Mateo Manje.* Tucson: Arizona Silhouettes, 1954.

McGee, W J "The Seri Indians," *Bureau of American Ethnology, Annual Report, 1895-1896,* Washington: No. 17, 1898.

McHenry, J. Patrick. *A Short History of Mexico.* Garden City, New York: Doubleday and Co.

Meighan, Clement W. *Indian Art and History.* Los Angeles: Dawson's Book Shop, 1969.

Meigs, Peveril. *The Dominican Mission Frontier of Lower California.* * Berkeley: University of California Press, 1935.

Miller, Max. *Land Where Time Stands Still.* New York: Dodd, Mead and Co., 1943.

Morrison, Roy F. *Trailering in Mexico.* Beverly Hills: Trail-R-Club of America, 1961.

Murray, Spencer. *Cruising the Sea of Cortez.* Palm Desert, California: Desert Southwest, Inc. 1963.

National Auto Club. *About Baja California.* Guidebook.

Nelson, Edward W. *Lower California And Its Natural Resources.* * Memoirs of the National Academy of Sciences, Vol. 16, Washington D. C. 1921. Riverside: Manessier reprint, 1966.

Nordhoff, Walter. *The Journey of the Flame.* (Novel) New York: Literary Guild, 1941. Reprinted in 1955.

Norman, James. *Terry's Guide to Mexico.* Garden City, New York: Doubleday and Co., 1965.

North, Arthur Walbridge. *The Mother of California.* San Francisco and New York: P. Elder, 1908.

_____. *Camp and Camino in Lower California.* New York: The Baker and Taylor Co., 1910.

Parkes, Henry Bamford. *A History of Mexico.* Boston: Houghton Mifflin Co., 1960.

Pesman, M. Walter. *Meet Flora Mexicana.* Globe, Arizona: Dale S. King, Publisher, 1962.

Pourade, Richard F. *The History of San Diego, Volume I: The Explorers.* San Diego: Union Tribune Publishing Co., 1960.

_____. *The Call to California.* San Diego: Union-Tribune Publishing Co., 1968.

Prescott, William H. *Conquest of Mexico and Conquest of Peru.* New York: Modern Library.

Rush, Philip S. *History of the Californias.* San Diego: Philip S. Rush, 1958.

Scammon, Charles M. *Marine Mammals and the American Whale Fishery.* San Francisco: John H. Carmany & Co., 1874. Riverside: Manessier reprint, 1969.

Shreve, Forrest, and Wiggins, Ira L. *Vegetation and Flora of the Sonora Desert,* 2 volumes. Stanford, California: Stanford University Press, 1964.

Steinbeck, John. *The Log from the Sea of Cortez.* New York: Viking Press (narrative portion of the Sea of Cortez), 1964.

Sunset Books and Sunset Magazine Editors. *The California Missions.* Menlo Park, California: Lane Magazine and Book Co., 1964.

———. *Mexico.* Menlo Park, California: Lane Magazine and Book Col, 1966.

———. *The Sea of Cortez.* Menlo Park, California: Lane Magazine and Book Co., 1966.

Timberman, O. W. *Mexico's Diamond in the Rough.* Los Angeles: Westernlore Press, 1959.

Toor, Frances. *New Guide to Mexico Including Lower California.* New York: Crown Publishers, Inc., 1965.

———. *A Treasury of Mexican Folkways.* New York: Crown Publishers, Inc.

Venegas, Miguel. *Natural and Civil History of California.* Originally published in 1757; first English edition in 1759.

Verissimo, Erico. *Mexico.* New York: Orion Press, 1960.

Violette, Paul E. *Shelling in the Sea of Cortez.* Tucson, Arizona: Dale S. King, Publisher, 1964.

Wortman, Bill and Orv. *Bouncing Down to Baja.* Los Angeles: Westernlore Press, 1954.

The cover of this book is Texoprint; it's a tough, durable plastic printing material. If necessary, it can be cleaned with a damp cloth and mild soap. The color pages are printed on Warren's Lustro Offset Enamel, dull finish. The text is printed on Patina; both of these papers feature a non-glare surface which permits excellent reproduction of both text and photographs.

Typesetting by Tech-Art Services, Riverside, California

The map which appears on the back cover of this book is an exact miniature of the new 3rd edition Baja Map by Mike McMahan. It shows roads, missions, resorts, Indian cave painting locations, major air strips, etc. This highly decorative five-color wall map (nearly 3 by 5 feet) is printed on tear-resistant Tyvek® from Dupont. Available in two editions: five-color shipped rolled, $14.50 postpaid, or in single-color Browntone printed on parchment-like paper, shipped rolled, $7.50 postpaid. Please order from Mike McMahan, 3131 South Figueroa Street, Los Angeles, Calif. 90007, (213) 747-4224.